RED PLUSH AND GREASEPAINT

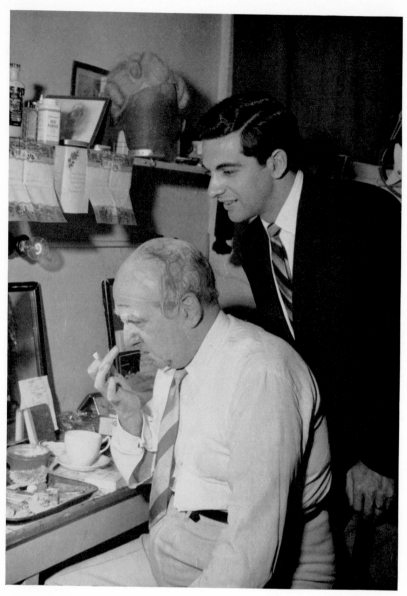

FRANKIE VAUGHAN watching the author put on a character make-up. (*Frontispiece*)

RED PLUSH AND GREASEPAINT

A Memory of the Music-Hall and Life and Times
from the Nineties to the Sixties

by

CLARKSON ROSE

Foreword by
JOHN BETJEMAN

Introduction by
VAL PARNELL

LONDON
MUSEUM PRESS LIMITED

First published in Great Britain by Museum Press Limited
26 Old Brompton Road, London, S.W.7

1964

© Clarkson Rose, 1964

Printed in Great Britain
by Ebenezer Baylis and Son, Ltd.
The Trinity Press, Worcester, and London
(R. 3175)

FOREWORD

I FEEL honoured to be asked to write a foreword to this book by my friend, Clarkson Rose. It is on a subject after all our hearts—music-halls, from the nineties to the present day, and it also embodies glimpses of the times, customs, manners, and way of life, in the background.

Many of us can remember those gilded halls of variety, which the title of this book suggests. We can hear the swish of the bar doors, as people come out into the auditorium, during the first turn—which is acrobats, or the dancing girls doing a can-can; we look up at the boxes and the plaster cherubs holding electric lights; we hear the crackle of peanuts in the pit; the stage is darkened, except for a standard lamp which illumines the grand piano, and then a single flood spotlights the artist—it is a serious turn, and we see tears run down old cheeks in the audience; excitement mounts as we reach the big names on the bill, who appear just before the interval, and last but one after it; the whole house rocks with laughter, or waits in breathless suspense for a well-timed joke; that rapport is established between the artist and audience—an intimacy and understanding which we remember all our lives. It is the true genius of music-hall, and something that television can never give us, and it differs from legitimate theatre in this way: in a play, it is the actors as a team who triumph or fail, and if there is a failure, the author and the producer can be blamed. A variety artist is his own producer, and, more often than not, his own author. If the variety artist cannot put his or her personality across in the first couple of minutes, all is up.

5

Music-hall, which, from the time of Sir Oswald Stoll, was re-named variety, is a hard school. It breeds a self-sufficient, clever and warm-hearted people. If its members were not all these things, they would never have made their names. Clarkson Rose and Olive Fox have kept the flag of variety flying for many years with their show, *Twinkle*, from whom, incidentally, many sterling variety artists have emerged—the most recent being Norman Vaughan. How many millions of waves must have thundered among the iron struts of piers below the seaside theatres of our coasts since the first production of *Twinkle*! Clarkie has known all the "greats" of variety in this century, and he is among them himself. He has the additional advantage—which is rare in his profession—that of being a writer of readable and interesting prose. Now read on. . . .

JOHN BETJEMAN

INTRODUCTION

I HAVE known "Clarkie" for nearly fifty years, as a writer, a comic singer, and a first-class revue actor, and with his vast experience of practically every branch of show business, coupled with his penetrative observation and journalistic abilities, I know of no one today who is better qualified to tell the story of the vastly changing scene of the times in general—and of the music-hall, in particular—from the old red plush days, down to *Sunday Night At The London Palladium*!

As a comic singer he was a notable contributor to the halls with which I was associated, and made big successes at the Palladium and the Holborn Empire with fine comic songs from his own pen—songs such as, "Back I Went to the Ministry Of Labour," "The Girls of the Old Brigade," and, to my mind, especially, a song called "I Had to Go and Draw Another Pound Out"—a particular favourite of mine.

Unlike some of the variety artists of his generation he was never content to rest on his laurels and on one or two outstanding successes, but was always ready with new material, and often I had to insist that he included in his repertoire songs that he thought it was time to discard.

He is as alert today as he was on one memorable Monday morning twenty-five years ago, when, at the band rehearsal at the Holborn Empire, Jimmy Gold—of Naughton and Gold—was taken ill. Clarkie was on the programme doing his usual act, but he immediately volunteered to stop in the theatre all day and fix up a double act with Charlie Naughton. To get Charlie practically locked up for a day was a feat in itself, but Clarkie did it, and that night he went on with Charlie, and "fed" him in superb fashion—so much so, that we kept the act in for the remainder of the week.

Another example of his quick reaction to an emergency was at the old Newcastle Hippodrome in 1928. A well-known animal act, Trubka, with his mixed bag of performing lions, tigers, leopards, pumas, etc., was on the programme. Clarkie's act preceded him, and he had to sing his last song in front of the house curtains, to enable the large cage and pedestals to be set and the animals to be poised for Trubka's act. One night, during Clarkie's last song, something went wrong with the fitting of the cage sections, and the section in the centre, which was practically flush with Clarkie's backside, fell inwards leaving a gap! The animals, immediately sensitive to any hitch in routine, became restive, and not only restive but they broke loose and fought with each other! The snarling and roaring was terrific; the audience became uneasy, and started to move; Mr. Alexander, the manager, rushed round to the prompt corner, and tried to attract Clarkie's attention. By this time, the audience were well on the move, when Clarkie, who had finished his last song, with supreme calmness, shouted to the conductor "Turn to number seven," and immediately he bravely and cheerfully sang another long song! By his action panic was averted, and the late George Black and myself not only sent him warm letters of thanks and congratulation but gave him a pass for life which gave him the freedom to enter any of our theatres whenever he liked!

Had he not devoted his time every year to his beloved summer show, *Twinkle*, in my opinion he could, with his brilliant material, have remained a variety star for far longer than he did. But, as he told me, he could never resist the call of the seaside in the summer, and he has undoubtedly proved that the music-hall's loss was the seaside's gain.

VAL PARNELL

CONTENTS

CHAP.		PAGE
	Foreword by John Betjeman	5
	Introduction by Val Parnell	7
I	Setting the Scene	13
II	Back to its Beginnings	19
III	First Experiences	25
IV	Trial Turn	31
V	Brogues and Dialects	36
VI	Comic Singers and their Songs . . .	46
VII	More Songs	51
VIII	Pubs to Palaces	55
IX	The Writing on the Wall	62
X	Some of the Greats	69
XI	More Greats	78
XII	A Jolly Lot of Fellows	87
XIII	Two Memorable Nights	92
XIV	Royal Occasions.	98
XV	Three-Course Supper—One and Six! . .	107
XVI	Ladies of the Promenades	114
XVII	Strike!	121
XVIII	An Old Date Book	126
XIX	That was Variety—That was! . . .	132
XX	Meet Mr. Showbusiness!	139
	Index	147

ILLUSTRATIONS

Frankie Vaughan watching the author put on a
character make-up . . . . *Frontispiece*

Facing Page

1   Ada Reeve 14

2   Dan Leno 15

3   Zena Dare 15

4   Arthur Roberts 15

5   Harry Tate 16

6   Harry Randall 16

7   Gertie Gitana 16

8   Robb Wilton 16

9   George Robey, in his early days . . . 17

10 George Robey, "The Prime Minister of Mirth" . 17

11 Herschel Henlere 32

12 Max Miller 33

13 Beryl Reid 64

14 Gracie Fields 65

15 The author installing H.R.H. Prince Philip as a
    Companion of the Grand Order of Water Rats 80

16 The Captains and the King forgather at the seventy-
    fifth Anniversary Banquet of the Grand Order
    of Water Rats 80

17 Val Parnell 81

18 Tommy Steele 96

19 Her Majesty the Queen visits Butlin's Pwllheli
    Camp and is escorted by Billy Butlin, O.B.E.,
    with his Director of Entertainments, Lieut.-Col.
    Basil Brown, T.D.   97

20 Millicent Martin   112

21 Frankie Howerd   113

Acknowledgements

The Author is gratefully indebted to the following for their
help in the preparation of this book: John Betjeman, Val
Parnell, Dennis Bartley, Mary-Jane Burcher, R. W. Swinson
(General Secretary of the Variety Artistes' Federation), the late
Barry Lupino (Curator of the Grand Order of Water Rats),
Lt.-Col. Basil Brown, Harold Vinter, Rodney Barrie, the
Daily Express, the *Western Mail*, the *Worthing Gazette*, Clifford
Henry, *South Wales Echo*.

The Author and Publishers wish to acknowledge with thanks
permission to reproduce photographs from the following:
1, Messrs. Bassano; 9, Lady Robey; 14, Baron Studios;
15, Joe Matthews of Matthews' News and Photo Agency;
17, Vaslav; 20, Christopher Smedley; Frontispiece, *Worthing
Gazette*.

CHAPTER I

SETTING THE SCENE

I HOPE the title of this book—*Red Plush and Greasepaint*—will
not make you think that it is just going to be another delving
into a misty—and sometimes musty—past, or that, because
I am a veteran, I write it with a grudge against the present—
because I assure you, I don't. Strangely enough, its writing
was first prompted by youngsters—and I will tell you how.

Some three years ago, I started writing a Newsletter for the
members of the distinguished variety brotherhood—The
Grand Order of Water Rats—covering our fortnightly lodge
meetings; these Newsletters not only dealt with the hap-
penings in Lodge, but often contained stories and miniature
biographies of some of the "greats" of the past, and I was
gratified—and, I suppose, flattered—by the warm reception
they received, especially from the younger and newer members
of the Order, many of whom had not been in the entertainment
profession very long. In these Newsletters, I often referred to
old-stagers of the music-hall and theatre, old customs, old
songs, and so on; the older members of our Order appreciated them—and, of course, I was pleased—but I was more
than delighted by the definite interest the youngsters showed.
"Why don't you write a book about it, Clarkie?" one would
ask. Another would come up with, "I did enjoy reading about
Wilkie Bard," or "I never knew Little Tich, Clarkie, but
having read about him in your Newsletter this week, I feel
I do now." Thus, it was very gratifying to hear young and

modern performers such as Tommy Cooper, Derek Roy, Cardew Robinson, Frankie Vaughan, Jon Pertwee, Norman Wisdom, Arthur Haynes, and Bruce Forsyth—to name but a few—urge me to write a book. "You are one of the oldest Water Rats, and more experienced in variety, pantomime, and summer shows than most people today," said our Scribe Rat, Harry Morris, to me, "and," he added, "I know you could tell us a lot—so why don't you do it?"

In passing, let me say that our Scribe is the Morris of the well-known Morris and Cowley duo—themselves veterans, and still a big hit on any programme in which they appear, whether it be the few odd variety weeks that are now obtainable, or on the newer media of television and radio.

I discussed the suggestion with a publisher, who seemed interested, and then, one day, the brilliant and erudite Ted Ray told me that he had been dining with that same publisher— "And, Clarkie," he said, "I told him that there was no one better or more qualified to write a book about our profession than you—so get on with it." This decided me—and here it is.

I do not claim that it covers the whole subject completely— it would require many volumes to do this—and, of course, it can only contain my own personal impressions and reactions, gained in a traffic of the stage of over fifty years, and an occasional fleeting picture of the times I have lived in since I was articulate. I do not believe in living in the past— except, perhaps, to reflect that it was very much cheaper— and I have tried not to look at it entirely through Clarkson Rose-coloured spectacles! There was a lot about the past that was better than the present, and there was also a lot about it that was a damn sight worse, both in our profession and out of it. I have no time for the "those were the days" brigade, because, frankly, it doesn't get anyone anywhere.

I think I knew where I was going—or hoped I was going— when I was about six years old. I was nurtured under an aura of Victorianism, and was always somewhat of a rebel. For

1.—ADA REEVE: one of our finest comediennes. An International Star and—at ninety years of age—still appearing in TV shows.

2.—DAN LENO: the immortal Jester.
Drury Lane's most famous pantomime
comedian.

3.—ZENA DARE: musical comedy star
before the First World War—and still
growing old gracefully in *My Fair
Lady*.

4.—ARTHUR ROBERTS: the famous
Victorian and Edwardian "Naughty"
comedian, whose spontaneous wit has
never been equalled.

years I was taught, and believed, that sex was something surreptitiously nasty and rather shameful, but I was never absolutely sure of this, and finally decided to find out for myself! In my childhood, my native town of Dudley was, I suppose, like all similar towns—a place of hidebound creeds and customs. It had its upper classes, presided over by the gracious Georgina, Countess of Dudley; its affluent middle classes, who lived in the big houses, and were almost a race apart; and it had its lower classes, whose children I often preferred to play with rather than with those of my own supposed station— that was the rebel in me, I suppose!

At Christmas time, and occasionally at other times, I used to accompany my mother and nurse, and other benevolent ladies, to the slums where they smugly dispensed soup and platitudes to elderly people, housed in hovels that were a disgrace to humanity. "The poor creatures don't always have enough to eat," a Mrs. Smythe-Browne or some similar named lady would say, "and this is good, nourishing soup for them." "Why haven't they got enough to eat?" I would ask. "We have got enough to eat at home." "Little boys should be seen and not heard," I was told. This remark, by the way, was the usual gambit used by any adult who couldn't understand a child's sensible question, and when my nurse said it to me one day, I replied "If I were seen and not heard, I should have to be deaf and dumb; do you think my mother and father would have liked a deaf and dumb child?" This caused the said nurse to tell me that I was a wicked boy, and not nearly so good as my brother Geoffrey!

Yes, this was the Dudley scene at the turn of the last century, and, as far as my adolescence goes, I was taught that the only way to heaven was via the Anglican Church; that Queen Victoria was a paragon of all the virtues—a fact which I always doubted; that W. G. Grace was the only cricketer in the country; that one's best clothes should always be worn on a Sunday; that the local theatre was rather a doubtful place, unless Wilson Barrett was playing there in *The Sign of the Cross*, or Osmond Tearle with his splendid Shakespearean Company, or, of course, the D'Oyly Carte or Carl Rosa Opera Companies; and that the music-hall was a cesspool of iniquity!

And yet, notwithstanding, my adolescence was happy. My parents were a strange contradiction of severity and tolerance, and I was lucky in the fact that we were a large family—there were brothers and many cousins all within walking distance of home. It was, of course, the day and age when children had to make their own pleasures: long walks, bird-nesting, tobogganing in the winter, drives into the country, river bathing, picnics and so on. There was no cinema, no radio, no television, and when someone mooted the idea of building a roller-skating rink in the town, it nearly caused a riot! There were highdays and holidays, of course. Chief among these were the famous Dudley Castle fêtes, for three days every Whitsuntide, with hair-raising acrobats and wire-walkers; the bands of the Grenadier Guards and the Besses O' The Barn: Lieutenant Lemprière and his balloon ascents, when the bands played—and we all sang—"Up In a Balloon, Boys"; and, at nights, the magnificent firework display with the set-pieces which at the time, I recall, depicted "The Relief of Mafeking," or "The Siege of Ladysmith." And, on Good Fridays, Pat Collins's famous fair pitched its tents, caravans and roundabouts. "Dreadful to think that the authorities allow that fair to be here, on this day of all days, with its blaring organs and its common coconut stalls. Don't you ever let me hear of you boys going there," Mother and Father would say. But I always did go—and enjoy it!

Then, of course, there were the annual seaside holidays which were generally spent in North Wales. These were carefree and joyous, with most of the day spent in the open air. Mother and aunts and other females trudging off a long way away to their bathing machines, and the males to theirs—Father and uncles in those hideous long costumes that hung around them like curtains, but which always showed their paunches! And the women, fully clothed almost—stockings

5.—HARRY TATE: whose famous "Motoring" sketch became a music-hall classic all over the world.

6.—HARRY RANDALL: brilliant comic singer and Drury Lane pantomime favourite.

7.—GERTIE GITANA: the Idol of the Halls and the British Public's own "Nellie Dean".

8.—ROBB WILTON: "The day War broke out!" Loved by the public and also by all his contemporaries.

9.—GEORGE ROBEY: in his early days.

10.—GEORGE ROBEY: "The Prime Minister of "Mirth".

and all—gingerly stepping into the water. The evenings were spent at the niggers or the pierrots if we boys had been good, or sometimes we had to go to the Celebrity Concerts and listen to Madame Melba or Tetrazzini—which we didn't appreciate! But on Sundays it was the same at the seaside as at home: church—and afterwards the church parade—and the rest of the day was rather dull, except for gargantuan meals!

Yes, they were good days. And, of course, everyone had the advantage of a golden sovereign being really worth twenty shillings in the pound. Can you imagine—cigarettes at three-pence for ten, in some cases twopence halfpenny? best assorted chocolates at fourpence a quarter? luscious Scotch or Severn salmon at two shillings a pound? Again, can you imagine a well-cut suit, made to measure, for from thirty to thirty-five shillings, the quality of which would now cost you from thirty-five to forty pounds? a cut off the joint with two vegetables, and a sweet, at a good restaurant, for from between one shilling and one shilling and sixpence? and can you imagine being able to post a bulky letter and putting only a penny stamp on, or being able to buy the *Daily Mail* for a halfpenny?

But times change—and it's a very different picture today, isn't it? This fact was strongly impressed on me after reading Sir Cedric Hardwicke's delightful autobiography *A Victorian In Orbit*. I was a member of the Birmingham Repertory Company, just before Sir Cedric joined, but never had the pleasure of playing with him, but I did work with, also teach, his delightful first wife, the late Helena Pickard. Sir Cedric's book is easily the best, frankest, and most self-revealing auto-biography of a stage personality that I have ever read. It is full of disillusionment, but a quaint sense of humour illumi-nates the bitterness. I often feel, as Sir Cedric does, and here I quote: ". . . It is an ugly age, and difficult for a man who started in the Edwardian era to keep pace with. . . ."

Yes, indeed, it is—but I do not despair; I loved the past, and I don't think we have replaced many of the great artists of those Edwardian days. On the other hand, why should we want to replace them? Surely is it better to leave them in the honour and glory of the niches they have carved for themselves in our memories? Rather should we rejoice that each generation gives us great artists, and that today we have stars like Peter Sellers, Max Bygraves, Harry Secombe, Peter Ustinov, Tony Hancock, Sir Donald Wolfit, Sir John Gielgud, Sir Laurence Olivier, Albert Finney, Peter O'Toole, Paul Scofield, Sir Alec Guinness—to mention but a very few.

And we also have Dame Edith Evans, Dame Sybil Thorndike, Vivien Leigh, Dorothy Tutin, Vanessa Redgrave, Anna Massey, Dame Flora Robson, and above all, in my opinion, the incomparable Dame Peggy Ashcroft—surely one of the greatest actresses the British stage has ever had?

And so, with these optimistic thoughts of the present and future, come with me on a trouper's trip, from the background of my childhood—those early days amidst the red plush, eventually leading to a much longer sojourn in the world of greasepaint.

CHAPTER II

BACK TO ITS BEGINNINGS

IF ever I win a substantial sum on the Pools, I think I shall buy a Supermarket, and turn it into a music-hall! Whether anyone would come to it or not I don't know, but I have an idea that if one could present real variety programmes, with modern performers—and *once* nightly please, not twice—one might attract a following. Who knows?

But that, of course, is only a dream, because the music-hall as we knew it, until just after the First World War, is dead. A lot has been said and written recently about the fact that the music-hall has returned to its beginnings—that is, the clubs and pubs, particularly in the north of England—but, on reflection, I cannot agree. There are some very lush pubs and clubs and night spots all over the North, but although some of them may be in the same locality as the old music-hall type of pub, they are as different from those old types as Dame Sybil Thorndike is from Shirley Bassey! True, they are giving employment to a lot of artists who are glad to accept the jobs and the excellent salaries that are paid. Indeed, some artists receive salaries that are larger than those they obtained in former variety days.

Whereas in the old days the audiences in the pubs actually came to a particular pub because there was an entertainment provided, these present venues are filled with people who are out for an evening's drinking or bingo or dancing, or even all-in wrestling at some places, but, above all, plenty of noise.

In most cases they couldn't care less about the performers or what they are doing. Many of the artists who have worked at these places—and, indeed, are grateful to be doing so—have told me of the agony they go through, especially artists who have to talk and patter, and many of them have also told me that it is impossible to raise any laughter whatsoever, or, indeed, any reaction, unless they use material that is outright unadulterated dirt. "How on earth do you cope with it?" I said to a well-known comedian, who recently completed a tour of these clubs and pubs, and whose work, as far as I have known him, is free from smut and filthy innuendo; "Well, I just go on and steel myself to do it," he replied, "and I tell the dirtiest gags I can rake up."

This, of course, is a vastly different atmosphere from the places where the true music-hall artist was born; I know they were sometimes rough and unkempt, but the artists themselves were native performers—of the earth earthy, if you like—and quite vulgar as far as domestic vulgarity goes. But this vulgarity was—as the late George Robey described it—"honest vulgarity," and some of it may have been lavatory humour, but it never touched on sex or vice. Moreover, they were the days of the comic singer, and when one reads the comic songs of that era, one finds trite, homely, and sometimes blatant lyrics—but you won't find any sex dirt. "The comic singer," the late Sir Oswald Stoll said, "built the music-hall," and the disappearance, almost without exception, of the comic singer, is, in my opinion, one of the reasons for the gradual decline of the music-hall. But more of this anon.

Please don't think the entertainment in those days was confined to the male artist only. Male entertainers were more plentiful, and, in passing, it is strange but true that they always have been, and practically remained in the most prominent position in this field, until the microphone era. The advent of this medium has, of course, brought us some excellent female artists, notably the incomparable Vera Lynn, and others like Anne Shelton, Alma Cogan, and Joan Regan.

But great artists like Bessie Bellwood, Nellie Farren, and Bessie Bonehill, all had early experiences in the clubs and pubs, and all went on to become great music-hall personalities. Nellie Farren, of course, was the toast of London when she was in the "Gaiety Burlesques," under Hollingshead. And later on there was the one and only Marie Lloyd, and artists like Harriet Vernon, Lil Hawthorn, and Alexandra Dagmar, who all served an apprenticeship of some sort in these places.

But, as a rule, the programmes in the pubs and clubs included far more male artists than female ones, and when the transition came and variety theatres sprang up all over the country, and later became organized into big circuits, such as Moss Empires, Barrasfords, the Syndicate Halls, the L.T.V., and in the North the MacNaghton Circuit and the Broadhead Circuit, it was the male artist and the male music-hall act that was predominant in the programmes presented.

The first variety theatres retained many aspects of the old pub concerts. There was, to my mind, always an atmosphere of a pub about the Oxford, the Tivoli, and even the London Pavilion. And, of course, music-halls like the Canterbury, and the Paragon in Mile End Road, were actually extended and modernized versions of their original edifices. The preponderance of the male artist in these programmes may, indeed, have helped, to some extent, the success of the female artists of the period, firstly because they were such a welcome change from the long succession of male acts, and secondly because to be a success in these surroundings, the woman who became a star had to be exceptionally accomplished and able to stand up to the many varied and excellent male performers in a programme. Can you imagine how refreshing it was, say at the Oxford, where sometimes there were over twenty turns, or acts as they call them today, after having seen Harry Randall and his comic songs; George Beauchamp and his comic songs; Paul Cinquavali, the great juggler; Eugene Stratton; a comedy sketch or a comic interlude from the Albert and Edmunds Troupe, or the Boissets, and then a

number would go up, and on would come Marie Lloyd or
Cissie Loftus! Believe me it was the signal for anybody who
was in those bars at the back of the hall, with their glass windows, from which you could see the stage, to go rushing back
to their seats. I remember an all-star programme at the old
Empire in Birmingham which had formerly been called Day's
Music Hall, and, indeed, the regular habitués still called it
that, when the bill included Little Tich, Tom Wootwell,
Dale and O'Malley, Van Biene, and George Lashwood,
among others—when on came Ada Reeve, and although the
other artists who preceded her had gone exceptionally well,
Ada Reeve electrified the audience, and, in modern parlance,
she stopped the show!

It says much for the early training of performers in the
primitive venues, that they took easily in their stride the larger
auditoriums and more ornate trappings of the new variety
theatres. But, of course, they had been trained in a hard
school, because the customers at the pubs demanded full
entertainment value; there were no such things as "free songs"
then, and, to the uninitiated, may I say that free songs are
published songs that can be sung by anybody—oh dear no!
in those days, an artist's songs were either written by himself
or for him, and were his own property, and could not be sung
by anyone else, except by special licence. Thus, if you wanted
to hear "Lily of Laguna" or "She Was a Dear Little Dicky
Bird", you had to go to wherever Eugene Stratton or George
Beauchamp were appearing. Occasionally, these songs would
be released by their owners for pantomimes, and a fee was
charged, but otherwise, they were the exclusive property of
the artist.

Mind you, these performers did have the advantage of an
orderly, if rumbustious audience, because there was always a
powerful personality, in the shape of the chairman, in charge,
and by "in charge," I mean he was more in charge in those
days than even Bruce Forsyth was on *Sunday Night At the
London Palladium*! His word was law; as a rule, he was a big,

florid man, with a large moustache; he sat at a table, smoked
cigars, and was plentifully supplied with liquor by the customers, which often resulted in his having a bulbous nose!
To be "in" with the chairman, was something to be sought
after, and to sit at the chairman's table, was almost the equivalent of being in the royal box! He always had a big, booming,
commanding voice; "LADIES AND GENTLEMEN—QUIET PLEASE!
DID YOU 'EAR ME? I SAID QUIET PLEASE!" . . . (and down would
come the gavel) "I NOW 'AVE THE PLEASURE TO HANNOUNCE
THE NEXT TURN—HENGAGED 'ERE AT HENORMOUS HEXPENSE.
PUT YER POTS DOWN AND SILENCE PLEASE, AND GIVE A BIG 'AND
TO YER GREAT FAV-OUR-ITE. . . . MISTER 'ARRY FREEMAN. . . ."
and on would bounce Harry Freeman, and sing three or four
of his inimitable comic songs. Harry, incidentally, was the
first King Rat of the Grand Order of Water Rats—a comic
singer who made his mark originally in the Birmingham
district, and was a particular favourite at the Old Steam Clock
music-hall in that city.

When the artist had finished, if the applause was insistent,
the chairman would say, "HORDER—HORDER! WOULD YOU
LIKE OUR GOOD FRIEND 'ARRY TO HERBLIDGE HERGAIN?"
Loud would be the clamour "YES—NOT 'ARF WE WOULDN'T
'ARRY!" "SILHENCE THEN"—and with that, the chairman
would turn and call " 'ARRY"—or sometimes " 'ARRY ME OLD
COCK SPARRER—KINDLY HERBLIDGE THE PATRONS WITH A
HENCORE." And these dyed-in-the-wool comic singers always
had a strong one up their sleeve to oblige with as a finish—
or what we call today—the "pay-off"!

You see, the difference between the pubs of those days,
and the clubs and pubs of today, is that the latter do not generally have a chairman, in the accepted sense of the term; they
have compères, and some of these are very good, but, good or
not, they have tremendous difficulty in keeping any semblance of quiet or even attention in these bingo-bewildered,
albeit very sumptuous, supposed counterparts of yesterday.
Only recently, a member of a well-known music-hall act, with

a nation-wide name—not only in places of live entertainment, but on radio and television—was, as he put it, playing in these clubs with the act because the money was good: "Far better, old chap, than ordinary music-hall money, and at some of the places we did 'enormous'. But then, there you are, we are a musical act, and don't talk." "Does it make a difference?" I asked, knowing perfectly well that it did. "You bet it does," he replied. "I don't envy any act that has to talk at these places—it's pretty hopeless."

You see what I mean? All that is a complete contrast to the atmosphere of the old pub music-halls or pub concerts. Comedians like Dan Leno and Wilkie Bard—to name but a couple—could patter to their hearts' content, and another contrast is that they didn't have to be dirty or smutty, and this in spite of the fact that the audiences in those days were, in the main, male, and were completely satisfied with their evening's enjoyment, consisting of a clay pipe, some shag, a pint of beer or porter, and some jolly comic songs!

CHAPTER III

FIRST EXPERIENCES

BEING fired with ambition, from the age of five, to go on the stage in any capacity whatsoever: melodrama, variety, the pierrots, or even the circus—and being, for a Victorian boy, what my parents and uncles and aunts called "a very forward child who wanted watching," I was, at eight years old, almost a walking encyclopaedia of the theatre and music-hall! I spent all my pocket money, and birthday and Christmas presents of money, on any professional paper or magazine appertaining to the theatre and music-hall, and I devoured them until almost the whole of my mentality was inoculated with what was happening, and who was who. I used to steal off surreptitiously from my home in Dudley to the local music-halls and theatres in the Birmingham district whenever I could, and, as twopence or threepence would buy a seat in the gallery, this didn't present any obstacles. Sixpence, indeed, would provide me with a gorgeous evening out; a seat at the Dudley Empire, a penny programme, a penny piece of fish, and a ha'p'orth of chips, and there was an ice-cream shop nearby where one could get an excellent ice-cream cornet that tasted like frozen custard, for a halfpenny!

Incidentally, when my parents were informed by our house-maid, who had been told by the young man she was walking out with, that I had been seen eating fish and chips out of a newspaper, they were simply horror-struck! I was called before them, and Mother said, "We never thought a son of ours would

be seen with common people in a common fried-fish shop—
and think of what the servants will think. What a disgrace
for us all!" Nevertheless, sixpence was indeed affluence.
Thus, between eight and ten years of age, I was making first-
hand acquaintance with most of the "greats" of the theatre
and music-hall.

My home was Victorian in almost every way, and, until my
parents' fortunes dwindled, and pennies became tight, the
house was typical of the age: large furniture, antimacassars,
aspidistras, Bibles, Prayer-Books, the *Morning Post*, *The
Family Herald Supplement*, and on Sundays roast beef and
Yorkshire pudding was as regular as Matins and Evensong,
and, before we kids went to bed on Sundays, we always had
to sing "Now The Day Is Over," to Mother's accompaniment
on a very large and heavily curtained piano which was slightly
out of tune, and as Mother's right hand did not always know
what her left hand was doing the result, to my wicked young
mind, was anything but God-like!

But although my father and mother were rigid, church-
going, and often very class-distinctive, they were, for Vic-
torians, fairly tolerant. Thus they would be mildly amused
when I came back from the niggers or the pierrots at the seaside, and reeled off some ditty that I had heard. Most of these
ditties were quite innocuous, but some of them did have broad
allusions, and to parents who were meticulous in manners and
behaviour, parents who would have had a silencer put on the
lavatory chain if they could have done so, some of the crude
vulgarity of these songs and ditties caused my mother to say,
"That will be quite enough, if you don't mind."

But, from time to time, when visitors came for a musical
evening—and musical evenings were, of course, part and
parcel of Victorian and Edwardian home life—they would
proudly tell the assembled guests that I would oblige—which
I would always agree to do, but when I reached a verse which
they considered doubtful they would immediately say as usual,
"That will be enough, thank you—we don't want any more,"

—and when I protested that there was another verse or more and that they hadn't let me finish, they were still adamant!

But there was one visitor—a Mr. Hartley, who would surreptitiously seek me out and encourage me. He was a bank manager and an excellent amateur actor and comedian, and he had a wonderful collection of the Era Annual Year Books, which contained photographs, data, and advertisements of everything to do with the theatre and music-hall in a particular year. I devoured these, as I devoured all the stage papers, and although I say it myself, I knew their contents almost by heart. "Where do you get all that rubbish from?" my father asked me one day, finding me in my bedroom, poring over them. "Mr. Hartley gave them to me," I replied. "Hmm, hmm," murmured Father, rather nervously stroking his moustache, and he left the room. I heard him go downstairs, and, with my nasty habit of eavesdropping, I leaned over the banisters and heard him enter the drawing-room and say to my mother, "Hartley encourages that boy in that stupid theatrical stuff far too much; we will have to speak to him—his mind's full of nothing but actors, actresses, and lowdown music-hall people." "Yes, my dear," I heard Mother say, "we must put a stop to it." Then there was a pause. "Push the door to, my dear—there's a draught coming from the hall," continued Mother. So the door was shut, and back I went to my room—and, in spite of the reprimand, continued to lap up all I could from the Era Annuals!

Probably my greatest thrill was in 1903, when Dan Leno came to open the Dudley Empire, and I was allowed to sell programmes after much badgering and cajoling of the manager. It was touch and go because, of course, there were plenty of boys who wanted to sell programmes on this occasion, quite apart from the usual staff, but I had haunted the managers and proprietors of the Dudley theatres for years, and it was almost with a resigned reluctance that the manager of the Dudley Empire finally agreed to let me. "Better let the little bugger sell them, else he'll bloody well haunt us all the time," said the

manager. Little did I think then that one day I should star
as top-of-the-bill at a music-hall in my native town—at the
Dudley Hippodrome. And when I was watching Dan Leno
I didn't think nor even dream that one day I should occupy
the chair he had occupied—that of King Rat of the Grand
Order of Water Rats, the most distinguished brotherhood of
world-famous music-hall artists, which, founded in 1889, is
now greater than ever.

Yes, 6 May 1903 was a day to remember, at any rate as far
as the Dudley Empire was concerned. Dan Leno was accompanied by his wife and also by Mr. Tom Pritchard, who had
been the presiding genius of the old tin Empire, and Mr.
Pritchard was, as usual, accompanied by Miss Violet Friend,
who was quite a well-known variety artist throughout the
country, but a particular favourite in Dudley. She was a
product typical of her age and of the variety stage of the era,
when big well-upholstered women and thigh-slapping principal boys were the vogue, and just as Tom Pritchard was a
superb showman, so was she. She could often be seen riding
at his side in his open carriage, through the streets of Dudley,
befeathered, bejewelled, and befurred, bestowing her bows
and smiles almost in the manner of royalty—and she certainly
was a great attraction there.

But, on this occasion, it was Dan Leno who stole all the
thunder. In fact the local paper reporting the show afterwards,
only mentioned Dan. It said, "An interesting programme of
talent included Dan Leno, who, with his inimitable drollery,
kept the audience in roars of laughter for half an hour . . ."
and there was no mention whatsoever of the names of any
other artists!

The Dudley Empire proudly announced that it was the
most up-to-date theatre outside London, and it had cost
eight thousand pounds—they charge that for a flat today,
don't they? And, moreover, it told the public that it had a
sliding roof, which "made it cool in summer and warm
in winter." I haunted it on many occasions, in fact I was

practically a weekly visitor, and it was there that I first saw that great comedian, George Formby, Senior, whom I have referred to at great length in a later chapter. On the same programme was Belle Elmore, better known later as the notorious Dr. Crippen's wife! Incidentally, the sliding roof was a mixed blessing—it didn't always work smoothly, and I remember one night, when watching the act of that excellent comedian, Cliff Ryland, a heavy thunderstorm made the audience very uncomfortable, and the sliding roof didn't respond too quickly to the emergency!

Reverting to Belle Elmore for a moment. She wasn't a top-rank artist, but, in her way, not bad—a blowsy, florid type of serio; and it may be of interest to recall that, after her disappearance, Dr. Crippen took Ethel le Nève to a Water Rats' Ball, and she was seen wearing some of Belle's jewellery! This fact did not escape the notice of certain ladies present who had known Belle Elmore, or worked with her; whisperings started, tongues wagged, and in short it was this ill-timed visit of Hawley Harvey Crippen to a Water Rats' Ball with his mistress, naïvely, and perhaps rather proudly, displaying her finery, that sparked off the inquiry which led to the results that you all know of.

I met Dr. Crippen once or twice; he was a quiet, meticulously mannered little man—a great frequenter of the music-halls, and, in fact, attended professionally several variety artists, and somehow I don't think he would have minded the fact that his name was to become a rather macabre music-hall joke, for years after his death, with many comedians, who, in sketches and otherwise, used the slogan, "Crippen was innocent!" It was a sort of pay-off to an outrageous happening or situation, as, for instance, one well-known comic, discussing in his patter his discomforts as a lodger, ended up by saying, "Cor blimey! You ought to see the landlady—what a face—Crippen was innocent!"

It is a curious fact that the house of this man, who was such a lover of the music-hall—39 Hilldrop Crescent, Campden

Town—should have continued an association with the variety theatre, because later a comedian named Sandy McNab occupied it, and he, too, became notorious; and later still part of the premises were used as a theatre- and music-hall-wardrobe, with which I was partly associated, and I cannot say that I ever felt any strange or eerie sensation when I went there with other artists for meetings and fittings.

CHAPTER IV

TRIAL TURN

THERE was a pub in Dudley called The Miners' Arms which was noted for its variety concerts, chiefly held on Saturdays. I looked older than my years, and had been pestering the landlord for several weeks to allow me to appear at one of them. One morning, sick of my badgering, he called me into the concert room and said, "Well, go on you little bugger, let's hear what you can do." Unaccompanied, I rattled off several songs and stories. For some time he sat there, with a grim and implacable expression on his face, and finally, he fetched his daughter in—she, incidentally, was an accompanist. "Show Elsie yer music," he growled, "and when you're ready, I'll come and 'ear you again." Elsie was a buxom, but very attractive young lady, and I think she took to me—and I certainly took to her—in more ways than one! She wasn't a Jack Byfield, by any means, but she took a great deal of trouble, and when I had finished this odd rehearsal, I said, "What do you think?" and the, by then, slightly dishevelled Elsie said, "You'll do—never mind what *he* says."—"He" was called in, and I went through some of my songs again, and this time my efforts were rewarded by admiring chuckles and other sounds of approval from Elsie—and then her father joined in with one or two grudging "Ha ha's." The net result was that he engaged me—and, moreover, agreed to pay me the sum of half-a-crown—untold wealth to me—to appear the following Saturday.

The great day duly came, and I was not only excited, but a little bit worried as to how I was going to get out of our house unnoticed and appear about half past nine—which would mean that I shouldn't get home until about half past ten. But, aided and abetted by the faithful housemaid, Sarah, this was achieved, and I duly presented myself at The Miners' Arms. What a thrill I got when I saw my name printed in soap on the glass window of the pub! Most of the pubs used this method of advertising their concerts in those days.

I was young, and very callow, and although bristling with the arrogance of youth, inwardly, there was a fearful inferiority complex.

I made my way to a small room, which all the artists shared. When I say "room," it was actually only a space, screened off from the back of the platform by a rather tatty looking curtain. Elsie brought some mugs of beer in for the artists, and I rushed over to her and started talking about my songs. "I'm not going to play for you, dear," she said, "I'm serving the booze. Here's the pianist, Mr. Shaw—just tell him what you want, love." And with a "See you later," and a wink, she disappeared. Mr. Shaw wasn't very helpful, obviously treating me as a beginner, and as of no account, and when I tried to explain certain points, he shut me up with a "That will be all right, my lad—I'm used to this sort of thing!"

At last my big moment came; I was duly announced, in my name of those days, by the chairman. "AND THE NEXT TURN IS A NEW-COMER, MAKING 'IS FIRST APPEARANCE WITH THESE 'ERE CONCERTS. LADIES AND GENTLEMEN—MISTER A. C. ROSE." And on I went, and I could feel that I was being examined from top to toe. The pianist messed up my introduction, and I was about a bar and a half in front of him during my first song, which was received in silence. I then, rather falteringly, began to patter, using some jokes that I had heard other comedians do in minstrel shows, pierrot shows, and the like. My timing and projection must have been weak, for the audience soon became restless. There was loud chatter, and

11.—HERSCHEL HENLERE: The Mirthful Music Master—International Star of three continents.

12.—MAX MILLER: the pure gold of the music-hall—who carried the traditions of the nineties right into the sixties.

the chairman himself was giving me deprecating looks. Suddenly, a voice from the back shouted, "Oo got you ready—speek oop?" which remark raised a far bigger laugh than any I had received, and it soon became pretty noisy.

Seeing my discomfiture, Ernie Garner, who was the star attraction, and a first-class comedian, who specialized in the Black-Country dialect, came on to the stage, and said, "Now then lads, 'ush oop—give the boy a chance; it's his first appearance, and he'll be all right—don't you worry." "Good old Ernie," they shouted. "Never mind good old Ernie," he retorted, "sup oop and listen." And then, turning to me, he shouted "Come on, boy—let 'em have it."

Ernie was a tremendous favourite, and had taken a great interest in me for several months, and this, coupled with his obvious paternal care, impressed the customers, which gave me courage and incentive. Turning to the pianist, I said, "Play number six." This was a song called "Does It Hurt You Very Much?" which I sang at breakneck speed, and this tickled the fancy of the audience, and I finished to shouts of "hencore," and the big-hearted Ernie came on and shook me by the hand, and, turning to the audience, said "I told you he was all right—you silly buggers!"

This is an opportunity for me to tell you about Ernie Garner; he was a natural comedian in every sense of the word—a big, moon-like face, a mobile mouth, a powerful voice, and the real vernacular of Staffordshire. He had songs of his own, and he also sang songs of which he had purchased the rights; so great was his appeal and popularity that, when the star top-of-the-bill at the music-halls in Birmingham and district failed to appear, through illness or for any other reason, Ernie was invariably called upon by the management to deputise. And, be it said, the absence of the star—whether it was George Robey, Little Tich, or Harry Lauder—made little or no difference to the business when Ernie was deputizing. At the Birmingham Empire, I once saw the manager walk on to the stage on the Monday night, and announce the fact that the great George Formby (the later George Formby's father—who, at that time, was one of the biggest draws in the country) was unable to appear, through illness. There were very audible "ohs" and "ahs" of disappointment at this announcement, but when Mr. Yates Gregory went on to say, "But in his place we have secured to deputize, your great favourite, Mr. Ernie Garner," the applause was deafening, and Ernie came on and did just what he liked with the audience for nearly half an hour.

His local fame rose higher and higher, and finally got to the ears of the head office of Moss Empires, who, although they had often called upon him to deputize on occasions like this, had never booked him outside his native heath. Ernie was subsequently given some bookings at other Moss halls, and it will always be a source of amazement to me that this great natural droll was not a very big success outside the Birmingham and the Black Country district. I saw him once at Liverpool and was astounded by the fact that although he went tolerably well, it was nothing like the reception he was accustomed to in the halls around his own dust-heap, and I still cannot understand it. Most people in our profession put it down to the dialect, but there again I am puzzled, because Scottish comedians, Irish comedians, Yorkshire comedians, Lancashire comedians, and even Welsh comedians, have found universal acclaim in English music-halls, but the Black Country or Birmingham dialect, although easily understandable—in fact, far more understandable to my ears than, for example, the broad Scotch of the great Neil Kenyon—never seems to have had universal appeal. At least, it didn't until quite recently when that splendid comedienne, Beryl Reid, hit the headlines—and is still hitting them—with her delicious Brummagem character study, "Marlene." As I write these words Miss Reid is making an outstanding success as "Marlene, The Maid" in the *Mother Goose* pantomime at that veritable home of pantomime, the Alexandra Theatre, Birmingham, but she has, of course, taken "Marlene" into all our homes via the radio, and, in doing so, has made everybody "Marlene" minded.

The fact remains that Ernie Garner, fine comedian that he was, never made the top grade, and yet his brogue and approach are almost identical with that of Beryl Reid's, which only goes to show what the new mechanical media can do, and has done.

Later, Ernie allowed me to use a couple of his comic songs, and just before he died, he sent me several scripts of his delicious "Black Country" stories, and it was due to him and his encouragement that later, when I became a bank clerk at Shrewsbury, I was able to add to my meagre salary from the bank by earning five bobs, seven and sixpences, and sometimes even half guineas, at smoking concerts and the like, all over Shropshire. This eventually led to my dismissal from the bank, when the manager and the bank inspector, having heard me at a couple of dinners, and then examined my books— which were far behind—decided that I was paying far more attention to comic songs than I was to their ledgers—which, of course, was quite true! They were indeed very generous, and gave me two months' notice, and during those last two months at the bank more engagements than ever came in, and it says much for the tolerance and good humour of the manager, Mr. Walker, that when I had the cheek one day to ask if I could go early, because I had a concert engagement at Wellington, he said: "With pleasure—and I hope you are good, because I recommended you, but, if I were you, I wouldn't do that 'Parsons' song, because there will be two clergymen present!" The song in question, incidentally, was called "Dearly Beloved Brethren," and told the story of a meek and mild curate visiting London, and the fate that befell him in such places as Short's, Romano's, and even in a music-hall! It was the property of that splendid comedian, Ernest Shand, who specialized in this type of song. One verse told of the curate's discomfort when he met a certain type of lady in Piccadilly— or, as he termed her, "one of the pilgrims of the night."

CHAPTER V

BROGUES AND DIALECTS

Scotland has produced some wonderful comedians, among them our first music-hall knight, Sir Harry Lauder. What a sensation Lauder was as he grew in stature on the halls, and what a packer of houses. He had a magnetism which I have seldom seen equalled, and an ability to put an audience in his pocket, whatever he did. His earlier songs were more of the comic song order than his later ones—songs like "I'm The Saftest Of The Family," "Stop Your Ticklin', Jock," and so on; but later, his pleasant and melodious voice turned to simple, homely doggerels, with very appealing and singable tunes such as "I Love a Lassie," and "Roamin' In the Gloamin'." But the material was not the reason for Lauder's success, and he wasn't even a funny man; but this gay, roguish troubadour, with the dominant personality, conquered any type of audience.

Neil Kenyon brought us some splendid Scottish character studies, and was a great favourite. Jack Lorimer (the father of Max Wall) was another excellent and breezy comic. But possibly the greatest all-round artist in the Scottish field, as far as the English music-halls were concerned, was Will Fyffe. He had come up the hard way, was a first-class actor, and had the two-fold ability of being able to make you cry, and the next minute make you laugh. Bill, as his pals called him, was a great friend of mine, and we were snooker rivals, and Bill was a very canny snooker player. He also had a splendid pantomime partnership in Scotland with Harry Gordon. Harry was another excellent comedian, who, like many of the other first-class Scottish comics—and when I say first class I mean it, was more popular in his native heath than he was in England.

The funniest Scottish comedian I ever saw was Tommy Lorne, who unfortunately died at the height of his fame; and Dave Willis ran him very closely. A forerunner of the successful Scottish comedians in England, was W. F. Frame, who might almost be said to be an early pioneer of Scottish humour over the English border.

But there have been so many fine Scottish artists. And the Scottish audiences are notable for their intense loyalty to their "ain folk." Year in and year out, you can find the same favourite faces in the big resident shows—names such as Jack Radcliffe, a brilliant all-round comedian, Alec Finlay, and, of course, latterly Jimmy Logan, Stanley Baxter, and Andy Stewart have been very popular.

We have been dealing with males, but we mustn't forget the Houston Sisters. I have always considered Renée Houston, who still makes her mark felt in plays and films, a truly un-harnessed genius. Today possibly the brilliant Margot Henderson is the most prominent Scottish artist to have found fame in English theatres. As I write these words she has been leading lady with the wonderful *Black and White Minstrel Show* at the Victoria Palace for the last year—and looks like stopping there for a long time yet.

I may sound like a heretic Sassenach when I say that the Scottish artists and managements have nothing to learn from this side of the border; and it is with respect I opine that there is quite a lot we could learn from them—and indeed, have learnt. I wonder what the late Fred Wyndham, whom I knew years ago, thinks when he looks down and sees the magnificent splendour of the Howard and Wyndham *Five Past Eight* shows, under the astute and able direction of that great gentleman of the theatre Stewart Cruikshank. There are few, if any, productions in England to equal them, but although the big Scottish stars have played a prominent part in their personnel, Mr. Cruikshank and his producers are also Anglo-Catholic in taste, and English stars such as Dickie Henderson and Max Bygraves have scored enormous successes in these shows— as did that brilliant artist, George Lacy, in their earlier *Half-Past-Eight* days. Aided by the dynamic direction of experts like Freddie Carpenter and Dickie Hurren, these shows are surely the pinnacle of lavish summer musicals. The major Scottish towns of Edinburgh, Glasgow, and Aberdeen are their strongholds, but we mustn't forget, in a lesser degree, the Gaiety Theatre, Ayr, first put on the variety map years ago by the lovable Ben Popplewell, and since then run from strength to strength by his two sons, Eric and Leslie, who year by year produce their notable *Gaiety Whirl* revues.

They belong to an older generation of theatre and music-hall managements who behaved like that, but, alas, they are a disappearing generation, or, to quote a song sung by Olive Fox, a great favourite at Glasgow's Pavilion: "There isn't a lot of 'em left!" And so we can indeed be thankful for Stewart Cruikshank and the Popplewells.

And now let us leave Scotland and look over the sea to Ireland. Many Irish comedians have made good in the English music-halls. To give examples, there was Pat Rafferty in the nineties and the early part of this century, and today there is that fine all-round comic, Jimmy O'Dea, who, although he only makes fleeting visits to England nowadays, has long been a favourite on our halls, particularly in the North, but his native Dublin never seems to tire of him—and no wonder, because he embraces nearly every facet of the comedians' art. And we must not forget Arthur Lucan and his immensely popular characterization, "Old Mother Riley," in which he was so firmly assisted by Kitty McShane.

Then, of course, there was Talbot O'Farrell, who popularized Irish songs and stories; his real name was Bill McIver, and he was known as Bill to his pals. He changed his name to

Talbot O'Farrell, dressed himself in shepherd's-plaid trousers and black coat, spats and patent leathers, and a grey topper, and immediately hit the public fancy. In fact, at one time, Talbot O'Farrell was the biggest drawing card in the country. He was a first-class showman, but at the height of his fame was inclined to be bombastic and full of bluff. Nevertheless, this façade he put on stood him in good stead for a long time, and, quite apart from this country, he was equally successful in Australia and America. He was fortunate and astute enough to be friendly with that fine pedlar of popular ballads, Lawrence Wright, who was, and is, not only a great publisher of songs, but, under the nom-de-plume of Horatio Nicholls, a fine writer of songs the public like, and who has an uncanny knack of gauging the taste of the moment. If one goes back over the Wright catalogues, one can see ample evidence of how "Lawrie" has cleverly kept in touch with the vast changes that took place, sometimes year by year, in public taste, and Bill O'Farrell owed a lot to him.

We now move to the Tyneside dialect, which I have always found most fascinating. One of the funniest Tyneside comedians I ever knew was J. C. Scatter. Today, his comedy would be classified as zany, but, like Ernie Garner of the Midlands, he was always in demand as a deputy for stars up North, and was immensely popular. A more solid Tyneside comedian was Adam Tomlinson—there was nothing zany about Adam. He had a cleverly worked-out act, and played very successfully all over the country. He retired before he need have done, and I believe he became quite prominent in local civic life.

There was also the one and only Jimmy Learmouth, a brilliant production comedian, copied by many, but equalled by none; and Frank E. Franks, who made a name for himself, not only as a revue comedian, but as a proprietor of shows. And lastly, but by no means least, there was Albert Burdon. When Albert first hit the headlines and audiences in Thomas Covery's *On The Dole* revue, he was a sensation wherever he went, and, in show circles, he was the talk of the business; so much so, that he attracted the attention of none other than the great C. B. Cochran. "Cocky" was seldom wrong in his judgements and direction, but it is my personal opinion that he made a mistake in trying to turn Albert into a West End comedian, or, in other words, make him "posh." I feel that had Cocky found a vehicle for Albert in which he could have been let loose to go his own individual way it would have been better. But Albert survived that experience, and is still surviving it today in no uncertain fashion.

In passing, I must mention Wee Georgie Wood, although nowadays he prefers to drop the Wee, and just be George Wood. He, too, is a Tynesider, but has never exploited the "hinny" brogue, and, of course, he has never needed to do so. This brilliant artist could, in my opinion, have made a hit with any brogue he had chosen— and he can speak them all like a native. Still, he is a "Hinny Boy", although he is known to audiences all over the world, in his splendid association in sketches with Dolly Harmer. One of the great qualities of Wee Georgie Wood's work was the fact that although he assumed the character of a naughty boy, his whole approach and projection was adult in every way, and at one time his audience control was astounding.

Wales, strange to say, gave us very few top-line music-hall acts, but for many years an excellent double turn—Ted and May Hopkins, who were very successful round the halls, as was Tom Jones, a Welsh comic singer, who sometimes appeared in traditional Welsh costume. On the lighter side Donald Peers, in my humble opinion, has had few equals as a tuneful and intelligent handler of good songs. Donald worked for years as a small act, and then suddenly hit the top in radio. I have been at the King's Theatre, Hammersmith when he was doing a broadcast, and you couldn't get near the theatre because of the crowds waiting to see him come out. Fame comes quickly and often goes quickly, especially in these days when a new pop singer arrives every few weeks or so, but

Donald remains the same, pleasant, competent, professional, and easy-to-listen-to artist that he was at the height of his fame, and, if I may say so, a new maturity has crept into his approach, which is very endearing.

Today, of course, Wales is more than represented by the irrepressible Harry Secombe, who, at the time of writing, is one of the biggest draws in the country; and Stan Stennett, with his own aeroplane, is flying high in more ways than one!

I hope I shan't start another War of the Roses—or even a war with Clarkson Rose—when I say that whilst we have had several Yorkshire artists who have been excellent, they have not been as numerous as the neighbouring Lancashire ones. The biggest name in Yorkshire comedians that I can recall in the past, was Tom Foy—a very quaint little man, with a broad Yorkshire brogue. He often made his entrance with a limp-looking donkey, and, walking down to the footlights, with the animal, would announce "I've coom." I saw him make a great hit in the Birmingham Theatre Royal pantomime as "Idle Jack," and he was a very prominent attraction on the music-hall bills of his time. Dick Henderson, too, came from Yorkshire, but never over-exploited the Yorkshire brogue; rotund, direct, and almost severe, he would roll off his patter at machine-gun rate, and then finish with a ballad, showing that he had a very pleasant singing voice. He was the father of that present day splendid artist, high up in the headlines— Dickie Henderson. Others I recall are Jack Lane, the Yorkshire rustic at the piano, and, of course, Sandy Powell, who again doesn't over-emphasize the Yorkshire dialect.

And then, there was the innocuous, disarming Jack Pleasants, who was fortunate in having a fine string of comic songs, one of which has been revived of recent years by many artists: "I'm Shy, Mary Ellen, I'm Shy."

On the other hand, Lancashire has given us a spate of top-line music-hall artists, far too numerous for me to mention them all. First, however, let me recall that wonderful and courageous comedian, George Formby. I am referring to the father of the later George Formby—and what a favourite he was, with his bronchial cough, his asides to the conductor, and his ridiculous songs, such as "John Willie Come On," "Standing At The Corner Of The Street," and many others. He was a universal favourite everywhere—just as popular in Glasgow, as he was in Manchester or London. His son, "young George," as I shall always think of him, came at a time when entertainment conditions were different, and he made a lot more money than his father did, and—to his credit let it be said—he never attempted to copy any of his father's mannerisms, but, with his ukelele and his broad smile, he sang his way to stardom and into a unique headline niche, until his tragic death a few years ago.

Another Lancashire lad is Ted Ray, whom I first remember as quite a small act—*Fiddling and Fooling* as he was billed on the programme—until the powers-that-be discovered how good he really was. He has a rapier-like wit, and few in our profession, if any, can equal him as an after-dinner speaker, and radio and television have put him where he deserves to be—right at the top.

And then we come to the mercurial Arthur Askey who came to see me when I was appearing at the old Liverpool Hippodrome nearly forty years ago, and nervously told me that one day he hoped to be as big a star as I was then—and as everyone knows he became, and still is, very much bigger.

He later bought several songs from me, which he sang on the Isle of Wight when he was appearing in Powis Pinder's popular *Sunshine* concert party at Shanklin. My own show, *Twinkle*, was his opposition on the pier, and I popped in to see him work several times. So impressed was I with his potentialities that I wrote to the great impresario, Julian Wylie, and told him that here was a star in the rapid making. Julian's partner, one of our most famous agents, Ernest Edelsten, telephoned me to say that they didn't want to waste their time coming down to the Isle of Wight on a fool's errand, and were quite luke-warm about the proposed visit, but so sure was I about

Arthur that, although I couldn't afford it, I offered to put them up at the best hotel at my own expense. They duly arrived and went to see Arthur's show—but came away unimpressed . . . which only goes to show that even top-flight impresarios and agents can and do make mistakes! It wasn't so very long afterwards that Arthur, in conjunction with Richard "Stinker" Murdoch, became a household name on the radio show *Band Wagon*—and from then on he has never looked back.

Julian Wylie wasn't the only manager that made a mistake about Arthur, for when I was at the Lyceum Theatre in 1937 Fred Melville came and asked me if I knew of a really funny short comedian who could partner me as "king" to my "queen" in the forthcoming pantomime. I said I did, and told him about Arthur Askey. He scratched his head, and tugged at his battered felt hat—a well-known mannerism of his—and said, "I don't know him, but I will take your word for it." Fred Melville often booked people on my recommendation as he had confidence in my judgement. I telephoned Arthur, who was very interested, and said that he would consider it for sixty pounds a week. I told Fred, and he said he couldn't pay that for an unknown person. Shortly afterwards, Fred came to me and said: "Clarkie, I heard a very good comedian with a grand voice and getting roars of laughter last night in one of those radio shows. You know Mr. Harry Pepper, so ring him up and find out about this comedian." I smiled, and told Fred who it was, "You could have had him for sixty pounds a week, Fred," I said, "but you won't get him for that now." And of course he didn't.

Another Lancashire comedian was "almost a gentleman"— Billy Bennett. He hit the headlines after the First World War, and was one of the few comedians that really made Queen Mary laugh. Billy was rough-hewn, but he had a stentorian Liverpudlian approach, plus excellent material that never failed, and he was just as big a success in the Society night spots as he was in the music-halls.

My favourite Lancashire comedian, and a great personal

friend, was dear Robb Wilton. He was a real character, with a wonderful sense of humour which always evidenced itself in spite of an almost unsurmountable series of family and domestic troubles and illness. I think my happiest pantomime experience, in over fifty pantomimes, was with Robb Wilton playing "Will Atkins," to my "Mrs. Crusoe," at the Theatre Royal, Birmingham. We were, so the public, the managements, and the Press said, the "ideal combination," and his slow, hesitant and quizzical methods, were a beautiful contrast to my quick retorts. Who will ever forget the humorous philosophy he brought us later, with his "The day war broke out . . ." —but, as I have said, Lancashire has given us so many wonderful artists that one could almost devote a whole book to them, and then find one had been omitted.

What, for example, is there left to say about Gracie Fields— the Rochdale lass who rose from small revues, to become the adored idol of the nation? Gracie's first Royal Performance was the same as mine—at the London Coliseum, 1 March 1928—and I still have a quiet giggle when I think of her seated in the middle of the revolving stage at rehearsal, calling me over, and saying: "Eee, Clarkie luv—how do you feel?" I told her I felt very apprehensive and nervous. "How do *you* feel, my dear?" I asked. "Eee—I feel as if I know nowt about owt!" she replied.

I think we all felt a bit nervous on that occasion, when one or two of those in charge, cloaked in a little brief authority as it were, were very busy telling us what we must do, and what we mustn't do, and that Queen Mary liked this, and King George liked that. The atmosphere that night was a little strained, and took a lot of breaking down.

Gracie had a protégé of whom she was rightly proud—he was Norman Evans. He had been a concert entertainer in the North, until Gracie spotted him and pushed him forward. What a delightful all-round comic he was. His particular forte, I would say, was being a master of mime, and his "Over the Garden Wall" sketch must surely go into the gallery

of music-hall classics. He subsequently became a very fine
pantomime dame, and, in fact, I would say that, of all the
newer school of dames who arrived about this time, he was
one who rigidly stuck to the older conceptions—the "bonnet
and shawl" type—adding, of course, his own up-to-date
material, and he was utterly believable. We became very
friendly, and once worked in Birmingham, in opposition
pantomimes, and every week, exchanged satirical, leg pulling
comments to each other. He has left a tremendous gap in the
pantomime scene.

We are leaving Lancashire with quite a lot unsaid about
many sterling Lancastrian artists, but the fantastic popularity
of that comparative newcomer to stardom, Ken Dodd, compels
more than passing mention. He started in a small way, but
when he did emerge he did so like a rocket, but unlike rockets
he doesn't look like ever coming down! In his second con-
secutive Christmas season at the Opera House, Manchester,
the advance booking office receipts, before he opened, were
colossal, and, in the words of one of the executives of the
Opera House, "will take a lot of beating." In fact, I should
think the only person who could ever beat them is Ken Dodd
himself! He is undisputed "Cock of the North," and de-
servedly so. His ingratiating style, his rapid and homely
patter, and his sparkling spontaneity, and then—almost as a
surprise—the melodious singing voice, mark an individuality
and personality that reminds me of the best old-time front-
cloth comics, standing alone in the modern scene.

CHAPTER VI

COMIC SINGERS AND THEIR SONGS

As I have already mentioned, Sir Oswald Stoll said that it was the comic singer who built the music-hall, and how right he was. I reiterate that although there are many factors for the decline of the music-hall proper, one of the chief ones is the disappearance of the comic singer and, with it, the comic song. The comic singers of those days, and also the ballad singers and chorus singers, were almost labelled by the songs they sang—the public whistled them, the hurdy-gurdies and the barrel organs ground them out in the street, the German bands played them, and you could hear them again and again on your musical-boxes or your phonograph records. The public never seemed to tire of them. The songs themselves may not have been great literary efforts, but they were very homely, and often very funny. These comic singers and ballad and chorus singers made a great impact on the halls, following the vogue of the "masher" type of song, and the "swell" songs and the jingoistic songs of the earlier music-hall, such as George Leybourne's and the Great Vance's. Leybourne's "Champagne Charlie" was, of course, probably the best known of these, and G. H. Macdermott's "We Don't Want to Fight, But by Jingo if We Do," was one of the famous diehard songs of the period, in the days, of course, when there *was* a British Empire!

In the same way, a little later, Arthur Reece's "Sons Of The Sea" did the same, and this, of course, was contemporary

with that splendid song "It's the Navy, the British Navy."
These titles must sound strange today, but those were the
days, of course, when the British Navy policed the seas, and
kept the oceans safe for most of the world!

In passing, one may say that this sort of patriotic song gave
way to a different type when Rudyard Kipling gave us "The
Absent-Minded Beggar." Do you remember the words—

> Duke's Son—Cook's Son,
> Son of a belted Earl,
> Fifty thousand horse and foot
> Going to Table Bay, etc.

And then there was "Tommy, Tommy Atkins, You're a
Good 'un Heart and Hand."

These gave place to songs with not quite so much bathos—
and that great comic singer, Billy Williams, treated the war in
a lighter vein in a song called "Since Poor Father Joined the
Terri-Torials, Ours is a Happy Little Home!" I was reminded
of Billy Williams a short while ago, walking through Oxford
Street, when I saw a young man in green corduroys and a black
velvet jacket, which only goes to show that things don't
change much sartorially, because Billy Williams was universally billed and known as "The Man In the Velvet Suit"!

Among other songs that the Boer War brought forth was
the very sentimental "Goodbye, Dolly Gray" and "Farewell,
My Bluebell." I have mentioned the Kipling songs, but
another war song at this time, in lighter vein, was the universally popular "Baby's Name," in which the chorus repeated the
names of famous generals and places such as Kitchener,
Carrington, Cronje, Spion Kop, Majuba, Baden-Powell, and
so on.

Wars always seem to keep Tin Pan Alley busy, but, clever
as the songsmiths were, when the First World War broke out
it was the sentimental British soldier who decided which should
be their marching song—and indeed the most popular song
this war produced—it was, of course, "It's a Long Way to

Tipperary." It was quite a fluke, actually, because "Tipperary" had been sung for several years, notably on the Isle of Man, as just an ordinary popular ballad—and indeed, it had no reference whatsoever to war. As a member of a pierrot troupe on the Isle of Man I had first hand experience of this song. It was written by a next-door neighbour of mine in the Black Country—Jack Judge, a popular local entertainer, who wrote an excellent chorus song called "How Are You?" at the same time. To eke out our small salaries, we pierrots could purchase quantities of these songs which Jack had printed himself at a cheap rate, and sell them to the customers on our pitch—or anywhere else we could. The songs were quite popular in the Isle of Man, and that was all; but when the boys turned "Tipperary" into their marching song-cum-signature-tune, that astute publisher, Bert Feldman, got cracking and bought the song from Jack Judge, and with his fine organization was able to exploit it, and it must have made a fortune for somebody!

That war inspired many songs which still live, such as "Pack up Your Troubles in Your Old Kit Bag," "Take Me Back to Dear Old Blighty," and Ivor Novello's "Keep the Home Fires Burning," and there were many others, such as a song I always heard generally sung by females, and treated as a patriotic exhortation. This was "We Don't Want to Lose You, But We Think You Ought to Go." I always writhed when I heard it sung by a certain well-known lady, knowing full well that she was living in the lap of luxury and was a frequent user of the Black Market of the period, and yet she could summon up a synthetic fervour to sing to the troops: "We don't want to lose you, but we think you ought to go, for your king and your country need you, you know," and as she reached those last words, "need you, you know," she would point her finger to the audience, and she only needed to have had a moustache to look exactly like the Lord Kitchener recruiting posters of the time!

Further, these songs occurred in a generation when we had

robust singers of songs—artists such as Florrie Forde, who, by merely singing a song and belting it out as only she could, could make it almost a best-seller; in fact, Florrie was regarded by music publishers in general, and Bert Feldman in particular, as the best bet in the business to plug songs, and had there been such a thing in her day, as the "Top Twenty Hit Parade of Pops," our Florrie would have been well up amongst the leaders. When you think of "Oh, Oh, Antonio," or "Has Anybody Here Seen Kelly?" you will know what I mean.

And at this time Harry Lauder wrote and created a song which is still sung all over the world today—"Keep Right On To The End Of The Road"—which he sang in the revue *Three Cheers* at the Shaftesbury Theatre, and on the night that he received the news of his son being killed he still went on in the show and sang it. That was typical of Lauder.

Another song of the First World War, which had nothing to do with war at all, but which, at the time, nearly rivalled "Tipperary" with the boys, was "There's a Long, Long Trail A-Winding," and like "Tipperary" it touched on the longing in the heart of every boy to get home to his sweetheart or his missis, or maybe his mother. There was one quite stirring American song which became very popular, called "Over There." It had rather a flamboyant and self-satisfied lyric, praising America's belated intervention in the War; nevertheless, it was a good song of its type, and our boys sang it, too.

The Second World War, possibly because it was such an entirely different type of war, didn't bring forth any really notable song—at least, not in the same way that the First World War did. Aeroplanes, panzers, doodle-bugs, and the like, cannot, and do not, inspire song-writers, but the boys did, of course, find their own songs—such as "Lili Marlene," and then, from Australia, we got "Waltzing Matilda." An attempt was made to plug a song called, "We're Going to Hang Out the Washing On the Siegfried Line," but I don't think it ever really made it.

Another song which had a short vogue was a tilt at Hitler

4

called "Run, Rabbit, Run." Then, later, there was a ballad called "There'll be Bluebirds Over the White Cliffs of Dover." On the other hand with the help of radio the sincere voice of Vera Lynn certainly not only made an impact, but gave the boys a song after their own hearts—"We'll Meet Again." There were, of course, several songs about the Army, the Navy, and the Air Force, such as "Roll Out the Barrel" and "Bless Them All," but few of them, as far as I can recall, took hold of the boys' and the public's imagination in the same way that the songs of earlier wars did. There was one song, of course, which lasted through two wars, and that was George Robey's and Violet Loraine's "If You Were the Only Girl in the World." Here again it is the warmth and love in the lyric, written by that splendid song-writer Clifford Grey, that made the appeal.

God forbid that there should ever be a nuclear war, because if there is, we are told that civilization won't survive, and if by a miracle a song-writer did emerge from a shelter in Tin Pan Alley, he would surely find no inspiration in annihilation.

CHAPTER VII

MORE SONGS

YES, indeed, it was the songs they sang and the way they sang them that made the reputation of many of our former stars; and here let us pause and not forget the song-writers. What a motley, and what a brilliant crowd they were. For example, one wonders if Eugene Stratton would have been so great without the wonderful collaboration he had with Leslie Stuart? I doubt whether there has ever been a song writer who could marry his work to the artists' abilities in the way that Leslie did for "Gene" Stratton, and Gene was always the first to acknowledge this. When you think of songs like "Lily of Laguna," "I May be Crazy," "The Little Octoroon," and "Little Dolly Daydream," to name but a few, you will realize what I mean. Leslie was supreme in his line, and everyone in the business will concede that he was unique in the fact that he always wrote real melodies—tunes that, in their very simplicity, were beautiful and easy to sing. He did the same, of course, for the musical comedy, "Floradora." Who will ever forget his "Tell Me, Pretty Maiden," or "Star of My Soul"? In fact no writer of his generation ever fitted lyric to music and music to lyric and the whole to an artist in the way that Leslie did.

Then again one wonders if Ella Shields, splendid artist as she was, would ever have attained her eminent position without "Burlington Bertie From Bow," written by her husband, Bill Hargreaves, who, incidentally, wrote many fine songs, including some excellent ones for that tip-top comic singer, J. W. Rickaby. Charles Osborne, George LeBrunn, Worton David, Henry Pether, Harry Castling, C. W. Murphy, and Bennett Scott, are just a few of the songsmiths who were invaluable to the artists they wrote for.

And then we come to one of the greatest song-writing partnerships the profession has ever known—Bert Lee and Bob Weston. There was hardly a star act of their day that they didn't write for, or at least who didn't want them to write for them, and they turned out some wonderful songs— probably a greater amount of real comic songs than any other song-writers have done. And what a couple of characters they were: Bob Weston, who wore glasses and used to blink like a frustrated butterfly whilst he was thinking out ideas—and he could get ideas from anywhere. He often told me that he got them whilst on the top of a bus watching people, and he confessed that he had many inspirations when occupying the smallest room in the house. Bert Lee was a short, quizzical northern character, and he had no high-falutin' ideas about inspirations or urges, and, at any rate during the last few years of their partnership, they became so inundated with work that they treated it as a business, and turned the respective front rooms of their houses into offices,—and, what is more—they kept office hours! They would meet every day, say at ten o'clock, at one or the other's house; Bob would sit at one end of the table, and Bert at the other. "What have you thought of?" Bert would ask. "I'm not quite sure," Bob would reply. "What have you?" "I'm afraid I shied away from thoughts of work last night," Bert would say, "I went out with some pals, and we had a bit of a do." "Enjoy yourself?" Bob would ask. "Eee, by gum, it were a real fine do," Bert would reply, relapsing into his native patois. "Eee, by gum, it were a real fine do," Bob would reflect, eyes beetling away. "That's a good title for a song, Bert." "I think you're reet," Bert would answer. And so the song, "Eee, By Gum, It Were a Real Fine Do" was written, and in a similar way one of their famous songs, "The Body In The Bag," was written after either Bob or Bert had had trouble with the neighbour's cat!

During the latter years of his life I was associated with Bert Lee at his war-time home in Llandudno, and I am proud of the fact that the last song he ever wrote he wrote in collaboration with myself. Meeting him on the pier one night, shortly after peace was declared, I said to him, "Bert, it's nice to see the lights up again, isn't it? And look, they've even got some ice-cream in the kiosk over there!" "Eh, well," he replied, "we had to get used to the war, so we've got to get used to the peace." "There's an idea there, Bert," I said, and I took him into the little office I had on the pier, and we decided to write a song with the title "It's Going to Take a Lot of Getting Used To." The next day, Bert wrote out a skeleton and gave it to me, and two days later we went down to the County Club, Llandudno, and he tinkled it out on the Club piano. "What do we do about this, Bert?" I said. "What do you mean?" he asked. "Well, it's a topical song—we ought to hire some rights of it while it's still hot." "Oh well, I'm too tired and too busy to bother about that—you see to it," he replied. I did, and rendered an account to Bert every three months. He was nothing if not keen on the business side, was our Bert, and although he died a rich man, whenever I go to Llandudno I pop up to the little church on the Orme's Head where we buried him, and I am sure I sometimes hear him shout: "Is there any more due from that song, Clarkie?"

The audience in those days never tired of hearing their favourite songs over and over again, and this also applied to favourite acts. That great cockney comedian, Gus Elen, always had to sing "It's a Great Big Shame" or "Wait Till the Work Comes Round" before they would let him go. In the same way Albert Chevalier could never get away without "My Old Dutch" or "Missis Henry Hawkins." Harry Lauder changed his material quite a lot, but it was very seldom he omitted "I Love a Lassie" from his repertoire. The immaculate Vesta Tilley, superb in every detail, had to do "Jolly

Good Luck to the Girl who Loves a Soldier" or "The Army of Today's All right," and nobody could imagine Charles Coburn without "The Man Who Broke the Bank at Monte Carlo" or "Two Lovely Black Eyes," and this is only to mention a few of the former stars.

That delightful artist, G. H. Elliott, had some wonderful songs, and I always thought he made a mistake in adding the great Gene Stratton's "Lily of Laguna" to his repertoire. George has often been credited with being the originator of this song, which, of course, he wasn't, but he was the originator and creator of such fine songs as "I'se A-Waitin' For You, Josie," "Sue, Sue, Sue," "I Want to Go to Idaho," and best of all, "I Used to Sigh for the Silvery Moon"—which audiences invariably demanded.

And this custom was continued right on until the advent of television. The public would have felt cheated had Marie Lloyd not appeared with her bird-cage to tell you what happened to her when she "Followed the Van." Will Fyffe's brilliant character studies always gave way finally to "I Belong to Glasgow," and I don't think the public ever thought they got full value for money if Gracie Fields didn't sing "Sally."

Nowadays, of course, things are different. Songs come and songs go, and it is seldom that one hears of a present-day song, if some of the current effusions are entitled to that name, lasting above three months.

CHAPTER VIII

PUBS TO PALACES

WHEN the transition from the public houses to the palaces of varieties took place, there is no doubt in my mind that a lot of the atmosphere of the old native music-hall was lost, probably, in most instances, for the good. But, in some cases, it was a gradual transition, because there were some very fine and intimate music-halls, and whilst they retained the theatrical atmosphere in every sense of the word some of the old pub intimacy remained. I think particularly of the Oxford, the old Canterbury, the Tivoli, Collins, the Pavilion, and the Met. And what wonderful value for money they gave you, long before the factory-like grind of "twice nightly" came in. You could go in at seven-thirty, and come out just before midnight, having seen anything from twenty to twenty-five acts. If there were acts you didn't want to see, or felt you could afford to miss, there was always a long bar at the back of these places, where you could go and have your drink, and peep through the window and see what was going on, and decide whether you wanted "another" or not. A full description of one of these wonderful programmes appears in a later chapter of this book.

But when Moss Empires and Sir Oswald Stoll started building their modern music-halls, this atmosphere vanished. Not all of the new theatres had licensed bars, but in those that did have them the bars were segregated, and if you wanted a drink or had to answer a call of nature you went out during the intermission, which, incidentally, I always thought must be rather heartbreaking for the conscientious and enthusiastic conductor, who often went to a great deal of trouble to arrange a good intermission.

And here let me say that there were many strong personalities among the maestros of the music-hall orchestras, who were part and parcel of the building, and some of them were so compelling that many people would stay especially to hear them. I faintly recall that great personality, Jacobi, of the Alhambra, and I later learnt a lot about him from his friends and relations. Then there was George Byng, also of the Alhambra, who afterwards took his musical knowledge to the gramophone companies and did a lot for His Master's Voice, and, may I say, was most encouraging to me personally, when I first made records. Later came Jimmy Sale, a great favourite of the ladies; Leon Bassett, with his little black Imperial; and, of course, the renowned Herman Finck.

These new palaces of varieties met a great need, and very soon, from being a show mainly for men, became an entertainment for the wife and family as well. Some of them, indeed, became fashionable social centres, such as the Palace in Shaftesbury Avenue. Here the music-hall programmes were magnificent in every way under the careful guidance and watchful eye of the redoubtable Charles Morton, who has rightly been called the "Father of the Halls." For many years now, of course, the Palace has been used for theatrical productions, but whenever I go to a show there I always subconsciously look back to the stalls to see if Charles Morton is sitting by his little table. Charles never missed a point—and many of the performers of that day owe a great deal to his knowledge and advice.

I remember Olive Fox's mother telling me that when she was engaged to appear there as a ballad-singer, Charles Morton said to her: "Listen, my dear; you have been associated with the classical concerts at the Queens Hall and the Albert Hall; your name—Florence Venning—is connected with them, so

I suggest you change your name for variety appearances."
Thus her name was changed to Ada Florence and she stayed
at the Palace for ten months in company with such artists as
Arthur Prince, the leading ventriloquist of his day, Ida Rene
and her "Rakes Progress," Datas, the memory man, Dutch
Daly and his concertina, Chirgwin, the renowned White
Eyed Kaffir, and many others.

Charles Morton was a kindly man, and he used to allow
Olive to sit on a little stool by his table in her school holidays,
and watch the programmes when her mother was appearing.
Incidentally, the Palace was the music-hall chosen for the
first-ever Royal Variety Show in 1912.

Here I must correct myself, and eliminate the words "music-
hall," because the term conjures up the earlier form of entertainment, whereas these later ones were variety theatres in the
full sense of the word. Take the London Coliseum for instance; after a shaky start with shows four times a day it was
transformed by Sir Oswald Stoll into what was undoubtedly
the ace variety theatre of the world—and this meant variety
in its fullest and most international sense. Year after year,
twice daily, Sir Oswald presented programmes which I don't
think have ever been excelled; they embraced every facet of
entertainment, and Sir Oswald Stoll was one of the first people
to induce the great actors and actresses from the legitimate
stage to condescend to appear in variety programmes—in
sketches or excerpts from plays. I have seen, and been on
programmes there that consisted of top-class variety stars: the
Diaghilev Ballet; Vesta Tilley; a sketch by the Irish Players
from the Abbey Theatre, Dublin, or alternatively, one by
Owen Nares or Fay Compton; Wilkie Bard; the cream of
the world's speciality acts, ping-pong champions, billiards
champions; David Devant; The Great Lafayette; Sarah
Bernhardt; Seymour Hicks and Ellaline Terriss; George
Robey; and, of course, the immortal Grock—and this is only
to give you an idea of the type of programmes which were
presented, month in and month out, at this wonderful theatre.

Generally speaking it was not, however, a favourite theatre
of front-cloth music-hall comedians, and I know of several
stars who disliked playing there. Nevertheless it was a most
sought-after booking with first-class acts and it gave them an
unimpeachable cachet, and the hallmark label. Artists were
proud to boast round the bars in the Salisbury or the Chandos
or the Cavour, that they had bookings for the Coliseum, and
I remember one incident when, having a snack at a popular
music-hall artist's rendezvous—Jones's, on the corner of
Leicester Square—a little comedian said to a much better-
known one: " 'Allo, boy, nice to see you. Are you working?"
"Yes," said the well-known comedian rather loftily, "I'm at
the Coliseum." The little lesser-known comic said: "Oh,
good—I was there three weeks ago." "You were at the
Coliseum three weeks ago?" queried the big man incredu-
lously. "Yes," said the little man, "the Coliseum, Kettering!"

The suburbs of London abounded with new and beautiful
variety theatres, where first-class twice-nightly programmes
were presented. The Victoria Palace, lately the home of the
Crazy Gang, earned high favour as a variety theatre under the
able direction of John Hayman, and was run in conjunction
with Sir Alfred Butt's Palace. In the provinces, of course,
twice-nightly variety theatres sprang up everywhere, and were
amazingly successful; Empires, Hippodromes, Palaces, and
what-have-you, thrived throughout the land. Away went the
older and rougher type of music-halls, which were either
demolished or re-built and re-furbished to become variety
theatres—there was hardly a town of any size in the country
that didn't have one of these. Possibly, the most famous of
all the provincial music-halls was the Argyle in Birkenhead,
under the direction, care, and—may I add—love, of that great
and astute music-hall magnate, Denny Clarke. I use the term
"music-hall" here, because, although Denny Clarke presented
as fine a weekly programme as could be found in the country,
the Argyle still retained something of its early origin—a pub.
I cannot name the number of artists that Denny discovered,

gave a chance to, and wisely booked up on long term contracts when they were beginning. The most notable example of these was Harry Lauder whom Denny Clarke had booked very cheaply for several years ahead, and even when Lauder was in the top flight with hundreds a week, he always honoured those early contracts, and I think I am right in saying that Denny appreciated the cheerful way that Lauder met his obligations in more ways than one.

And so the variety theatres up and down the country rode the crest of the variety wave, and the great stars of the day became household names in every town. But from about 1912 onwards, a change was evident. Sir Oswald Stoll had the idea that his theatres should have more culture and more uplift, and in attempting to raise the tone he introduced musical acts and classical singers into his theatre, who, from a variety point of view, savoured of the highbrow. The red-nosed comedian didn't vanish entirely, but his appearances were less frequent. A rigid censorship was kept by the Stoll Office on all material used in their shows, and in consequence the influence of what I will call the "concert" type of act, made the variety programmes lose something of their former rumbustious appeal. Sir Oswald himself kept a watchful eye on his theatres, and had a definite programme of visits. On Monday afternoons he would always be in his box at the London Coliseum, and when, later, he added the Alhambra to his circuit he always attended the first evening performance there. On Thursday evenings he always went to the first house at the Chiswick Empire; and likewise, on Saturdays, to the first house at the Shepherds Bush Empire. His visits to his provincial halls were not so frequent, but he certainly didn't neglect them. Moreover, if he took an interest in an artist he would—and did—send for that artist to go to the office. He once sent for me after a matinée at the London Coliseum, and, in that quiet, but definite voice, objected to a line in one of my songs. He had some strange ideas, and perhaps I can best illustrate this by giving you the verse as I sang it in the afternoon, and the altered verse as I sang it at night. It was a song all about different types of girls, and this is how the original went—

> Any girl looks all right in a bath marble white
> With beautiful bath salts like peaches,
> But the queen of my soul has to stand in a bowl
> And wash down as far as it reaches!

Sir Oswald didn't like the last line of the song at all, and thought it was "common and vulgar," and so I promised to alter it. And here I have to thank him for his correction, because the alteration was a far bigger laughter-raiser, and here it is—

> Any girl looks all right in a bath marble white
> In beautiful bath salts she'll frolic,
> But the queen of my soul has to stand in a bowl
> And do what she can with carbolic!

As it so happened, I was called upon to deputize at the Chiswick Empire during that particular week at the Coliseum. Sir Oswald Stoll heard me sing the new version and afterwards he sent his manager—that cheery bloke, Jack Persich—round to tell me that he was very pleased.

That little incident will give you some insight into the strange kinks of this music-hall magnate—a man who started in a small way, in primitive music-halls at Cardiff and Liverpool, and who rose to become, at one time, our greatest variety impresario. Nevertheless, I still think that his rather fixed views on variety, and his extreme censorship, took a lot of native life out of variety, and sometimes, indeed, I have seen programmes in Stoll theatres which included four musical acts, and that, in twice nightly variety programmes of eight or nine acts, was too much—and was not pure music-hall.

The other great music-hall combines, such as Moss Empires, the Barrasford tour, the Syndicate Halls, the L.T.V., the Gibbons' halls, and, in the provinces, the MacNaghton

Circuit, and the Broadhead tour, didn't succumb to this new
wave of respectability that Sir Oswald Stoll was infusing into
his theatres, and neither did the great independent music-
halls, of which there were many, and, in consequence, in my
opinion, their programmes were livelier and more truly representative of variety.

There are various reasons given for the decline and fall of
the British Empire and Palaces of Varieties, and there *are*
many reasons, but I often think that it was Sir Oswald—
with his methods, and without, of course, any intention or
thought of doing so—who was the start of it. Nevertheless,
the variety profession owes a lot to this very great man. He
stood for respectability, both in his public and his private life;
right to the last he would arrive at his London Coliseum office
in top-hat and frock-coat, which he rigidly adhered to long
after other magnates had discarded the Victorian garb. I
think he had a superstitious streak in his nature, which, to
my mind, was very pleasant and understandable, and it was a
fact that whenever he opened a new theatre, his mother was
always in charge of the box office. He believed she brought
him luck, but whether she did or not, she herself was almost
a "mother" of the music-hall, and I can still picture her in the
Coliseum box-office, beautifully dressed in her own dignified
way, and sometimes almost coquettish in the way she wore
her jewellery.

CHAPTER IX

CHAPTER IX

THE WRITING ON THE WALL

DURING the First World War, and immediately afterwards, the variety theatres boomed, as indeed, did most places of entertainment. The Alhambra, for instance, with the "Bing Boys," was almost a club for the lads on leave, and so, in many ways, was the dear old Holborn Empire and the Palladium. And then, towards the thirties, came the slump which perhaps started with the General Strike of 1926. Then followed increasing unemployment figures, and the general depression, and big financial readjustments. Music-halls and theatres are, naturally, the first to suffer in times like these, but I am not sure that this was the only reason for declining attendances. I think it must be admitted that many of our stars of that time became very lazy regarding their material. Bear in mind that there were dozens of variety theatres within a ten-mile radius of the London Coliseum, and many artists, particularly the stars, would be playing at the London Palladium, for example, and doubling with a suburban hall, or, on occasions, even with two suburban halls. Thus, if you visited the Palladium and later on went to the Lewisham Hippodrome or the Kilburn Empire, you were quite likely to see several of the same acts, and, generally speaking, they would be doing the same material that you had seen them do at the Palladium! Not only that, but the artists themselves, secure in the possession of long and good contracts, hung on to their successful acts, and did not change their material at all. Consequently, month in and month out, and year in and year out, you not only saw the same artists, but you saw them doing the same acts!

Anent this there is an amusing story about the very quick-witted Malcolm Scott. Malcolm was the brother of the famous gunnery expert, Sir Percy Scott, a cultured man and a brilliant artist, with a lofty, and, at times, almost haughty approach to all and sundry. He became famous for his delicious study of Katherine Parr, and, except in his early pierrot days, when he was with that fine firm of Adeler and Sutton, I never heard him do anything else but his Katherine Parr act.

The story goes that after the first performance at the Palace on an umpteenth return engagement Charles Morton said to him: "When are you going to change your act, Mr. Scott?" and, sticking out that aggressive jaw, Malcolm hissed: "When the Brothers Horne change theirs!" To the uninitiated may I explain that the Brothers Horne had played their well-known "boxing" routine for years and years!

Malcolm was more supremely indifferent to audience reaction than any variety artist I have ever known. I remember being on a programme with him at the Hackney Empire in the twenties when Sir Oswald Stoll was fostering me, and had billed me almost as prominently as Malcolm. Malcolm was closing the first half of the programme, and here let me say that Hackney Empire audiences were not exactly what we will call Malcolm's meat! No, indeed, Hackney much preferred the more raucous and down-to-earth comedian, and Malcolm's Katherine Parr reminiscence didn't appeal, especially to the Hackney galleryites who had the annoying habit of eating peanuts throughout the performance. The constant cracking of the nuts and the rustling of the bags could be very disturbing. During Malcolm's act this cracking and rustling became particularly loud, and towards the end he stepped forward, and, in his sibilant, cultured tones, said, "Mister and Missis Hack-er-nee—it is obvious that you don't appreciate anything about that illustrious lady, Katherine Parr; to be fair to you, I didn't think you would, and I have often asked Sir Oswald Stoll not to send me to Hack-er-nee; so I do assure you it is not my fault I am here. They love me at the London Coliseum, but it is quite obvious that you don't at the Hack-er-nee Empire. However, don't despair, my good friends; very soon a young man is coming on, whom you will simply adore. His name is Clarkson Rose; he has a loud voice, some very obvious comic songs, and I am sure you will love him. I am going now, but, in the meantime, get on with whatever you are eating, and if there is not a pea at either end —you've been done!"

Malcolm took a great interest in my work, and he promised me that I should have his Katherine Parr costume when he retired. In the meantime he lent it to that excellent light comedian, Ambrose Thorne, with the following typically Scottish instructions; "When you have done with it let Clarkson Rose have it; he is just my height, and when his bust develops, it should fit him perfectly!" Eventually Ambrose gave it to me. I still wear it for certain items, and such was the quality of the material and decorations that it looks as good today as it did when Malcolm first wore it!

But, to get back to the question of the return visits of artists to halls and acts that they had been seen in over and over again. It certainly began to have its effect on attendances, and the following story, to my mind, is a sad, but funny, reflection on the situation.

Olive and I presented our show *Twinkle* one Sunday at Parkhurst Prison, on the Isle of Wight. The stage manager was a good conduct prisoner, who did his job well and asked me if I would try and help him when he came out of prison— which he told me he would be in a few months' time. When that happened he came to see me when I was appearing at the Empress Theatre in Brixton. After a short chat about what I could do for him I asked him if he found London very different after his sojourn at Parkhurst—and bear in mind that he had been there for seven years. "Not very much, sir,"

13.—BERYL REID: "Marlene" to most of us. A comedienne of the new school with the old school punch.

14.—GRACIE FIELDS: needs no other description than "Our Gracie".

he replied, "in fact, I didn't notice a great deal of difference since I went away; the roads are still up in Oxford Street, and Lorna and Toots Pound are still at the Palladium!"

Yes, indeed, it was obvious that the public were getting wise to the fact that they weren't having a great deal of variety, and were seeing the same old stuff again and again. And yet there is a strange contradiction in this attitude. They loved their favourites, and, as I have mentioned earlier, they had labelled their favourites with certain songs and acts, and when some of them did bring new acts the audiences were really disappointed if they didn't have an old number. It was a difficult position, not only for the artist, but for the management. The chief trouble, in my opinion, was the fact that so many of them had long, watertight contracts. One could understand the reluctance of an artist who had found big success with certain songs or acts to change them, and even if they did find replacements many of them suffered from the fear that they were quite sure it wasn't as good as their true and tried successes. But here again, in some instances, managements were to blame, especially later on, and many artists could tell of a similar experience to one that I had.

I had played a certain prominent suburban variety theatre for the first time, which in itself was strange because I played theatres time and again on the same circuit for years—sometimes with very quick return dates—but had never yet played this particular hall. However, it so happened that I was lucky enough to score a big hit. A very short time later, much to my surprise, I was transferred from a week at a provincial hall back to this same suburban theatre where I repeated the act I had done previously, and luckily for me, they still liked it. Judge my surprise when a short time later I was again transferred from another hall back to this self-same suburban hall, and so I prepared an entirely new act. I received a nice welcome on my entrance, and I was very pleased with the reception of the new act. When I say "very pleased," I would here add that only an artist himself really knows if he has gone over well or not. Whatever your friends may tell you, whatever praise you may get from your fellow artists or some of the staff—you know, if you are a performer at all, whether you have hit 'em, or whether you haven't. And I was quite sure that not only had I done well, but that the audience were pleased that I had given them a new offering. However, much to my amazement, a prominent representative of the booking department came round after the first performance on the Monday night and said: "Very good, Clarkie—but we wanted you to do your old act. Will you please put it in for the second house?" "But," I protested, "this is my third visit here in a very short time. I wanted to give them something new, and surely they liked it?" "Oh yes, it was all right, but we would like you to do your old act—it suits the programme better. . . ." So where are we?

So much for the effect of the same faces and the same material, week after week, at our variety theatres; but, alas, there were other causes, because, after the Second World War, following on the war-time boom, a lot of new managements—and other ones who should have known better—started putting on cheap and rather tatty revues. Then came the all-male shows—many of them very good, notably the famous "Splinters," with those sound artists, Hal Jones and Reg Stone; unfortunately, bad imitations of them were done to death. And finally the striptease and the nude shows arrived, some of which had a vogue for a time, and, in fairness, some of them were very well done with an artistic angle that excused—in some degree—the nudity; but inevitably there came those with no semblance of entertainment about them except rather nauseating nakedness without any finesse. The striptease shows increased in number and steadily decreased in quality, and some of them were just blatantly sordid and dirty. So it was only to be expected that the exodus of the families from the variety theatres increased by leaps and bounds. I hope I shan't be accused of being a prude and a moralist— I assure you that I can appreciate the nude figure of an attractive woman as well as anybody, but not necessarily in a wholesale exploitation of it on the stage of a theatre. Some of the nudes that appeared in these shows would have been far better fully clothed because, had it not been sad, it was almost laughable to see some of the extraordinary shapes and sizes that were exposed. I suppose they gave some excited pleasure to certain male members of the audience, but, of course, they were quite unable to maintain the standard of a theatre presenting a variety entertainment; not only that— I am sure that many of them closed those very theatres.

The reader may say: "Well, striptease shows are doing very well in London at the moment—and in some provincial towns." With that I must agree. There will always be a market for shows like these, where men with a certain outlook can go and, presumably, enjoy themselves. In the same way there are the key-hole clubs and other pornographic entertainments, and this narrative is not going to comment on them apart from mentioning them in connection with the decline of the music-hall. In any case, the decline was there for all to see, and thus the seed of slime was sown when television arrived.

Let us face the fact that people were generally able to see far better entertainment in the greater comfort of their own homes than they could see in a tatty music-hall. There is nothing more depressing than a music-hall that is fading and on its last legs. Many of them were in need of paint, reseating etc. In one, I recall, the gilt-and-plaster cupids and cherubs decorating the private boxes were chipped and broken. In another music-hall I saw the plaster figure of a goddess, as part of the proscenium decoration, which couldn't have been Venus de Milo, because not only had she no arms, but she was minus her left breast and one leg; and on the other side whatever effigy it was holding a lamp had been beheaded! This was typical of the condition of many halls towards the end. Some managements did make brave attempts to resuscitate variety, and some met the conditions by reducing the orchestra, the staff, and the lighting. Possibly they had no alternative, but, of course, it didn't help to make a place of entertainment inviting.

Has television been one of the causes of the decline? Yes, of course it has. In fact, it has altered the whole aspect of entertainment, especially for artists, and it is simply no good scoffers talking disparagingly about the "goggle-box" and other such names, because the goggle-box has dealt live entertainment a devastating blow; not, in my opinion, a death-blow, but, nevertheless, a severe one. On the other hand, television has given a lot of work to artists of every description, and—what is particularly gratifying about it— it has found work for many people who had faded out of the variety world, and it is a joy to see them popping up in all sorts of television shows.

But there are, of course, a vast number of people whom it has hurt considerably. What has happened here in the variety world, happened earlier in America. There is no variety there now, as we knew it, and what there is is confined to the night spots, and places like Las Vegas. "It's only a passing phase," said a well-known variety artist, in a certain club recently. "I am sure variety will have a come-back." To this I replied: "And where will it come back to?" How can it indeed, when variety theatres have been closed, pulled down, or turned into offices or television studios in such a wholesale fashion? No, over the doors of the variety theatres, as we knew them, can be written "ICHABOD."

CHAPTER X

SOME OF THE GREATS

I CANNOT attempt to deal with all the "greats" of the past and present in variety, and I am only going to write about a few that I have known, worked with, and learnt from. I will start with George Robey.

When I was an office boy in Birmingham George Robey was my idol. I would spend my tea money and any odd tanners I could get hold of and go and see him whenever he came to the halls or the theatres of that city, and at pantomime time, although I lived in Dudley, I would pretend to my parents that I was working late in order to pop down to the back door of the Theatre Royal and glue my eyes to a crack in the door so that I could watch him make an exit or an entrance.

Robey was a strange man—a martinet in a show—but he always replied to my letters, some of which must have seemed trivial to him. At his best I think he was undoubtedly the greatest front-cloth comedian of his day. It has been said that he was very "blue," and I have contradicted this time and again in lectures at Rotary Clubs and other places as well as in newspaper articles. He certainly believed in and practised "honest vulgarity," but I never heard him say a smutty word or line in his work, although, of course, he was a master of the unsaid! In that rich, rasping voice he would crack a perfectly innocent joke, and wait, and when the loud laughter of audience reaction came, he would indignantly swish that cane, and raise those eyebrows and say: "Kindly temper your merriment with a modicum of reserve!"

But he was not only a tip-top music-hall artist—he was a great comic actor, as he proved in many revues at the Alhambra and the London Hippodrome, notably with the "Bing Boys," and, of course, his incursion into Shakespeare was an event in every way. I modelled my early pantomime work a great deal on his, and always told him so. I was very proud when I was appearing at the Manchester Opera House in a pantomime in the thirties when he came to a matinée, and at the end of the performance addressed the audience from his box in very complimentary terms about my work.

As a pantomime dame, he was unsurpassed; and another remarkable thing about Robey was that he was one of the few performers who was a star—and remained a star—from his very first appearance. He was never second to anyone, and his famous title of "The Prime Minister of Mirth" does him no more than justice.

Stars have always been very particular about the prominence or otherwise of their billing. A long time ago, Marie Lloyd was negotiating an engagement at the London Palladium—where she had always previously been the sole star attraction at the top of the bill. Policies had begun to change, however, and Charles Gulliver had started having three or four big names at the top. The militant Marie would have none of this; they tried to persuade her to have two well-known artists sharing the honours with her for this particular engagement, but she was adamant: "No," she said, "I am sole top of the bill—or not at all. There are only two artists I would ever share the headline with—Little Tich or George Robey."

I unhesitatingly think that Marie Lloyd was the greatest variety comedienne I have ever seen. I didn't know her well in my early days, but I did get to know her fairly well for a short while after the First World War. No music-hall artist has ever endeared herself to the hearts and affections of audiences—particularly London ones—more than Marie did; what an artist she was, in every way. In a smart gown, sparkling jewellery, with those attractive protruding teeth and a wink that could convey a wealth of meaning, she could charm and devastate with her talent and her sex; and then, for her next item, gone would be the fashion-plate and glamour and back she would come as a bedraggled cockney housewife, telling us in inebriated tones how she became "One of the Ruins that Cromwell Knocked About a Bit"! Her handling of lyrics was dynamic, and it didn't have to be a particularly brilliant lyric for Marie to infuse an untold wealth of meaning into it; as, for instance—

"I always 'old with 'avin' it—if yer fancy it,
  If yer fancy it—that's understood
  And if drinkin' makes yer fat—I don't worry over that,
  'Cos a little of what yer fancy does yer good!"

I think you will admit that this is not a masterpiece of song writing, but there were, of course, other verses and choruses about things that a fleshly minded person might fancy, but when Marie huskily rolled out those trite lyrics, as only she could, with her tongue in her cheek she devastated the audience with laughter, long before she reached what were supposed to be the funny couplets!

Like George Robey, Marie had the reputation of being "blue." This was an injustice; saucy—yes, Rabelaisian—yes, but never dirty. And it was a great shame that, because of this reputation, she—the most brilliant music-hall comedienne of her day, and possibly of any day—was omitted from the first Royal Variety Performance which took place in 1912 at the Palace Theatre. These performances, incidentally, are erroneously known as Royal *Command* Performances; actually, they are no such thing, and I will touch on this subject later.

Highly incensed and upset, Marie retaliated by holding a "Public Demand Performance" at the Crown in Peckham. Of course one realized that the powers-that-be had to be very careful and keep a strict censorship on the programme—

particularly because this was the first time that royalty had honoured the variety profession in this way—but the great Marie Lloyd was quite capable of toeing the line, and, as this particular royal show was supposed to represent the cream of the variety world, she should, undoubtedly, have been a number one choice, and—good as this first royal show was, and it *was*, indeed, a brilliant show—in the absence of Marie, it still lacked a rich drop of the cream.

But in some way it was as well that she didn't appear, because, as some will recall, Queen Mary was seen to turn her head and study her programme when the great Vesta Tilley appeared in male attire—it was stated that Her Majesty disapproved of women in men's clothes—all the same, the very *joie-de-vivre* of Marie might have conquered the Queen.

Many years later I lived at Golders Green, two roads beyond Marie Lloyd. Her house was a landmark and known to all, but the road I lived in was a new one and unadopted, and if one got a taxi late at night in the West End it was difficult to explain to the driver where it was, but I found that if you told him it was two turnings past Marie Lloyd's house, no further explanation was needed. "Oh! Marie's house on the corner," the cabby would say. "Right ho, Guv! What a card, eh? I took her 'ome the other night, and she invited me in for a noggin—bless her 'art. There's only one Marie!"

This fact was indeed proved on the occasion of her funeral. All London seemed to be there in every sort of vehicle to follow their favourite's mortal remains to the grave, and no artist from the theatre or music-hall has ever had a bigger funeral. At one time it was stated that the crowds were larger than those for the funeral of the much loved King Edward VII —or "Teddy," as we all called him.

One of the most remarkable music-hall artists I ever knew was Bransby Williams; remarkable in the fact that he was not only a number one variety performer, but a first-class actor, and, by his great artistry and personality, he was able to bring the characters of Charles Dickens, and many others, to the halls. When one considers that his act was a highly intelligent one, which dealt in good literature and required the close attention of an audience, it is worthy of note that Bransby was just as successful at the roughest provincial and suburban music-halls as he was at the sedate London Coliseum.

To the strains of an old-world gavotte he would make his entrance in knee-breeches, square-cut tails, waistcoat and cravat, standing with quizzing-glass elegantly poised, his head, with its luxuriant locks of black wavy hair, flung back, and in cultured rich and round tones he would commence his act. Bransby's elocution was perfect; he spoke in the lovely lilt of the true Shakespearean actor, and, strangely enough, this was in complete contrast to his ordinary conversation off-stage which was deliciously cockney. Although he specialized in Dickensian studies, he had many other acts—all of them superb—and, of course, he was a brilliant mimic. Many times I have asked him in his dressing-room to bring back the voice and mannerisms of former famous personalities and artists, and, in a trice, one forgot Bransby Williams was there, and the room was peopled with Dan Leno, Arthur Roberts, Herbert Campbell, Henry Irving—and sometimes, even, Disraeli or Mr. Gladstone!

Unlike some of the stars of his day he didn't resent new-comers, and he took a great interest in me. I was on the bill with him at the Coliseum, when I was able to afford my first motor-car. Proudly I took him to the stage door to show it him. He put his head inside and said, "Good, me boy—it's splendid; but you must have a nice carpet for Olive." And with that he went to his own car which was parked nearby, took out his carpet, and put it in my car. "A present from Bransby," he said jokingly.

I learnt a wonderful tip from him, which has been very helpful. One day, watching me removing my make-up with grease, he saw me wash afterwards in hot water, and commence to dry. "Silly boy!" he said, "you've had hot make-up on your face; you've just opened the pores with hot water, and now you are going out. You should do as I do . . ." and he showed me that, after he had done the hot water wash he ran cold water, and thoroughly bathed his face—and particularly his neck and throat—in it for three or four minutes. "Always do that, me boy," he said, "it closes up the pores, and keeps the throat muscles taut."

They say the test of a man's character is his reaction under setbacks and failures. When Bransby Williams took a company to Canada to play Dickens and Shakespeare he lost nearly all his life's savings. He had the opportunity of closing down—when theatres over there did close down—and sending his company back. Instead of that, he paid them for the full term of their engagement and brought them home in style—and in doing so he left himself nearly on the rocks.

It was a privilege—although a sad one—when his partner in so many plays, Kathleen Saintsbury, asked me to give the oration at his memorial service in 1962, at St. Paul's, Covent Garden. I felt my tribute was clumsy and pedestrian; consequently, I was surprised and very proud when Sir Michael Redgrave, who was there to unveil the plaque, said: "Well, ladies and gentlemen; after Mr. Clarkson Rose's wonderfully perceptive and sincere tribute to Bransby Williams, there is nothing left for me to do but unveil this plaque to his splendid memory." Dear Bransby Williams—a great artist, and a great man, and almost, at times, a little boy who wouldn't grow up —that was part of his lovable charm.

No greater contrast of personalities could be found when we jump from Bransby Williams to Harry Tate. Harry was an extraordinary man in many ways, with his own particular sense of humour—a sense of humour which, today, could be described as "taking the mickey out of the establishment." He will be chiefly remembered, of course, for his famous sketch, "Motoring," and here again, he took the mickey out of motoring with unbridled hilarity. Can anyone who saw him ever forget that wiggling and twitching moustache which he used to convey pomposity, and then to deride pomposity.

Harry's work and approach was pure burlesque, and—as true burlesque should be—it was so near the real thing.

The stories of Harry Tate are legion, and they are told whenever pros foregather, and, be it said, the new generation of pros are always anxious to hear them. He really did see the funny side of everything.

Typical of him are two Tate-isms which I always enjoy. He and his great friend, Robb Wilton, had decided to have a holiday on the coast together for health reasons, and had agreed to eschew alcohol, or, in other words, to go "on the wagon." They started off one morning from London with Harry driving, and at Crawley he stopped at a well-known hostelry. "What are you stopping for, Harry?" asked Robb. "Thought we'd just pop in and have one," said Harry, "we've got a long journey in front of us." "But aren't we on the wagon, Harry?" demurred Robb. "Yes, I know," replied Harry, "but we don't want to be morbid about it."

And another delicious one was when, towards the end of his days and when things weren't too good for him, he was playing at the Glasgow Empire—never a particularly enthusiastic ground for English comics. It was the first performance on the Monday, and Harry was, shall we say, a wee bit under the weather. Suddenly, a loud Scottish voice rang out from the stalls: " 'Arry Tate, yer drunk—go hame." Harry's expressive eyes boggled, he walked down to the footlights, his moustache went to right angles, and he said, "I beg your pardon?" The voice repeated, "I said ' 'Arry Tate, yer drunk—go hame.' " Harry turned to his assistant in the sketch and said, "I told you we were—we should never have come!"

I could go on and on—as many others could—with these Tate-isms. It may not be generally known that, long before he specialized in his ridiculous sketches, he was a first-class mimic. Like his great friend, Robb Wilton, his sense of humour never deserted him. He had known great affluence and prestige, and he had known otherwise; and no greater tribute of his innate decency and niceness could be found than in the affection of his wife, Maud, and his son, Ronnie. Ronnie, who has the same sense of humour as his father, is one of our most popular Water Rats, and never tires of relating anecdotes of his dad—he laughs like a drain at them, even now!

It is fitting that I should now turn to Robb Wilton, whom I have already mentioned earlier in this narrative. He was a dear friend of mine, and one of the most solid and reliable characters in our profession, and, in a profession where back-biting and envy of others can be prevalent, I never heard Robb say a nasty thing about anybody. When I received the invitation to appear at my first Royal Performance I was playing with him in pantomime in Birmingham, and he was more overjoyed for me than if he had had the invitation himself, and, bear in mind, he had not yet received that honour— although, of course, he did shortly afterwards. For many years, he had had a difficult and, at times, very sad domestic life, but he was a wonderful husband, and when he lost his wife, Florrie—who had partnered him in so many of his earlier sketches—he was a lonely man, but even then could always see the funny side, and typical of this is the following story.

One Sunday evening he and little Nat Mills—of the famous Nat and Bobbie Mills partnership—were invited out to play snooker at the hospitable home of the B.B.C. producer, Richard Afton. Nat had not yet recovered from the loss of his wife, Bobbie, and he could be very sentimental about it. They were bowling along in the car to Hampstead when Nat turned to Robb and said: "Well, Robb old son, here we are, going out for an evening's enjoyment; both of us lonely men, trying to snatch a bit of innocent recreation. I have lost my Bobbie, and you have lost your Florrie. Never mind, Robb, they know that although we are going out to enjoy ourselves, we shall be thinking of them." "Shall we?" asked Robb lugubriously. "Yes, Robb, we shall. And, don't forget,

whilst we're playing snooker Bobbie will be up there (pointing skywards) watching me, and Florrie will be up there
(again pointing skywards) watching you." "S'truth!" exclaimed Robb, "you've spoilt my whole bloody evening."

On Sunday, 21 June 1959, the Lord Mayor of Liverpool—
Robb's home town—was invited by the Grand Order of
Water Rats to be present at the Empire Theatre when we un-
veiled a plaque to Robb Wilton's memory. The reigning King
Rat—Johnnie Riscoe—performed the ceremony, and I was
privileged to recite, afterwards, my humbly written tribute,
as follows—

> We're gathered here today, my friends, with homage in our
>   hearts,
> To pay our loving tribute to a man of many parts,
> A son of this great city—who adds another page
> To the history of the famous sons it's given to the stage.
> Ted Ray—Arthur Askey—Frankie Vaughan, to name but
>   three
> And thousands more—both great and small—but none more
>   loved than he.
> His British sense of humour was the sort that never hurt,
> Native wit—and gormless, too—but never any dirt.
> He left us just two years ago—his going left a blank
> In the Order of the Water Rats—in which he reached the rank
> Of King—the highest honour—one that only comes to those
> Who've earned the love and confidence of all their fellow pros.
> So our present King and all of us, have come here to acclaim
> His memory—and on a plaque perpetuate his name
> That all may be reminded of this city's famous son
> Robb Wilton—who has left us such a legacy of fun.
> Yes—we in Liverpool can say, with pride, without a doubt:
> Show business had a lucky break—the day when Robb broke
>   out!

CHAPTER XI

MORE GREATS

A NUMBER of veterans make the mistake of saying "Oh—those were the days"—and, in doing so, almost seem to say that none of the present-day artists can compare with them. That, of course, is quite absurd, and, in my opinion, based on a vast experience—we have never had a better bunch of entertainers than we have today. Although I admired, loved, and learnt a lot from many of the old stars, with few exceptions they cannot be compared with the brilliance of the present-day line-up. Only in one particular do I think that present standards fall below the past ones—and that is in the lack of characters, the lack of individuality, as opposed to massed talent. Your current male entertainer, more often than not, appears in the latest mohair or alpaca dinner-suit, is quite immaculate, and generally has very good material—but they do tend to be somewhat of the same pattern. However, the vigour and the attack of the great ones of today—stars such as Bruce Forsyth, Max Bygraves, Norman Wisdom, and Tommy Trinder—and the splendid way in which they cope with the giant octopus of television that gobbles up material nightly, is nothing short of brilliant.

The old-timers, of course, weren't trained to this sort of situation, and, although some of them could have done, most of them couldn't have even begun to tackle it. Robey possibly could have in his heyday, and so could Will Fyffe, Ada Reeve, and that great American favourite with British audiences—

R. G. Knowles, and also, perhaps the greatest and richest spontaneous wit the theatre and variety stage has ever known, Arthur Roberts.

Tommy Trinder, to my mind, is one of the greatest compères that can be found for any sort of function. His pugnacity, tenacity, and capacity for the quick retort, is unique. I have seen him heckled—and I have been sorry for the heckler —I have never seen him fail. I went to see him work in his early days, when he was with Jimmy Hunter's *Follies* on the Brighton Palace Pier. He wasn't as polished as he is today, but the quality was there for all to see. I was looking for a comedian to come to Eastbourne for the following year, and after seeing Tommy I persuaded the managing director of the Pier at Eastbourne, Mr. Owen Taylor, to come and see him with me. "This man will be a sensation with *Twinkle*," I told "Teddy" Taylor. Teddy was a nice chap, rather inclined to be pompous, and very conscious of the fact that he was an old Bensonian and that he was also virtually the dictator of the destinies of Eastbourne Pier. After watching the performance at Brighton I said to him: "Well, what do you think?" With a curl of the lip, and a supercilious smirk, he said: "Clarkie, you must be mad! This man would be no good at all—he's far too common." "Common be damned," I replied, "he's brilliant." And how wrong Teddy Taylor was is proved by Tommy Trinder's meteoric rise very shortly afterwards—and I was only sorry that I was the loser.

He is proud of his position as chairman of Fulham Football Club, and brings his penetrative powers to the job. The Fulham directors are really lucky people in having a chairman who is not only a knowledgeable enthusiast, but who can always pour the oil of good humour on troubled waters.

And now, let us turn to the ladies for a moment—and begin with "Gert and Daisy," otherwise known as Elsie and Doris Waters. Surely one could call them the cockney forerunners of "Coronation Street"? They carved a definite niche for themselves in the music-halls, and this, they will admit, was greatly aided by their broadcasts—in fact, to my mind, broadcasting is their greatest media, and I have never heard them give a bad performance.

Blessed with a tremendous sense of humour they overcame many difficulties and snags in their early days on the halls, and this sense of humour is perhaps exemplified by an advertisement they put in a trade paper when they were appearing at the Victoria Palace. It read roughly something like this—

ELSIE AND DORIS WATERS
This week: Victoria Palace—First Turn
Thus proving that it is possible to die more than once!

I have written many songs for them, and have always been proud to hear them sing them.

There have been many great favourites among music-hall stars—names the public clamoured to see, and who could fill a theatre, but when it comes to idols, as opposed to favourites, there really have been very few. Among the women we had Marie Lloyd, Vesta Tilley, Florrie Forde, and Gracie Fields— to name but four—but there has been no greater idol of the halls than Gertie Gitana. No artist has ever belonged more to the music-hall than Gertie. Irrespective of her talents she was universally loved and, indeed, entirely possessed by the stalls, pit, and gallery of whatever hall she appeared in. What was the secret of her great success? I doubt if anybody could really answer that question correctly. She wasn't pretty, and yet she mesmerized all and sundry with that long black hair and simplicity of approach, plus obvious sincerity, emphasizing that she believed in all she was singing and doing. She was, indeed, that "nice girl next door." She sang about "Nellie Dean"—and she *was* "Nellie Dean"—and as they listened, the women in the audience imagined *they* were "Nellie Dean," and the men wished that they were the one who sat and dreamed by the "old mill stream" with her! No wonder her husband, that great variety agent, Don Ross, was inspired to produce that fragrant parade of veterans "Thanks For the Memory."

15.—The author installing H.R.H. Prince Philip as a Companion of The Grand Order of Water Rats. With him are (*left to right*) TED RAY, His Royal Highness, King Rat ARTHUR SCOTT, Preceptor CLARKSON ROSE (10 March, 1960).

16.—THE CAPTAINS AND THE KINGS FORGATHER at the seventy-fifth Anniversary Banquet of The Grand Order of Water Rats. *Back row:* George Doonan, Tommy Trinder, Johnnie Riscoe, Bud Flanagan, Ted Ray, Clarkson Rose; *sitting:* Albert Whelan, next to Georgie Wood, George Elrick; *front row:* Charlie Chester, Ben Warris, Cyril Dowler.

17.—VAL PARNELL: the great variety impresario, and the inspiration of *Sunday Night at the Palladium*.

And what can we say about the indestructible Sophie Tucker? It has all been said before and will all be said again. When I heard Ethel Levy introduce the song "Some Of These Days" in her *Hallo Ragtime* at the London Hippodrome in 1913 I little thought that she was giving a preview of a song that was to become the signature of one of the greatest favourites America has ever sent us. Sophie's command and authority is amazing. "Life Begins at Forty" she used to sing, and, as far as she is concerned, it could begin at any age.

Sophie is more than a great artist—she is a great woman; her generosity and kindness are boundless. And how kind and unselfish she has always been to fellow performers. I had the unenviable job of following her act on one occasion, when we were at the Palace Theatre in Manchester, many years ago. After the Monday morning band rehearsal I said to her: "Sophie, you are an idol in this town, as you are everywhere, and I have got to come on after you sing "Yiddisher Momma" —and late in the programme at that. I shall simply die on my feet!" "Don't you worry," Sophie said in that deep voice, "leave it to me, Clarkson." At the conclusion of her act that night the audience practically went mad—they yelled and shouted for more. And the yelling and shouting for their favourites in those days, may I add, makes the reception of some of the present-day stars, with all the hysterical squealing and swooning, pale into insignificant contrast. My number went into the proscenium frame; they were still calling for Sophie. She stepped through the curtain, held up her hand to quieten them down, and said: "Yes, yes, I know—but time marches on. Now listen, folks—there's a young man coming on, whom your Auntie Soph likes very much" (and with this remark she gave a wicked wink!) "and you're gonna like him too, and what is more, I'm gonna stand at the side and watch him with you. So come on, folks, give a big hand for my good friend, Clarkson Rose." And then, bless her, she went and stood at the side of the proscenium, and led the applause— and, of course, I couldn't fail after that.

6

Another example of Sophie's good comradeship occurred at Shanklin Pier in 1932, when I had engaged her to appear as my Sunday guest artist. The dressing-room accommodation was primitive and very limited, and when Sophie arrived, with the indispensable Ted Shapiro, I had to explain to her that there were some rather rickety wooden steps leading down to her dressing-room, which was slung underneath the pier girders. "Don't worry about that," said Sophie, "I will come into your room." And with that she had her American trunk put half-way across my room and a little curtain slung up round her half of the room. After her act that night, we were finishing the show on a concerted scena, and Sophie insisted on appearing in it, and me giving her some hastily-thought-out lines to say, and she actually appeared in the finale line-up wearing one of my comedy bowler hats! A very great woman indeed.

Talking of piers brings me to Gillie Potter. Before he became a notable feature in variety programmes he was a contemporary pierrot with me, under the Wallis Arthur banner. It was Gillie, of course, who put the mythical village of "Hogsnorton" on the map. In the pre-television era thousands of listeners would switch on their radios just to hear that cultured voice say "This is Gillie Potter speaking to you in English." That phrase sums up Gillie's outlook. He was a brilliant humorist, and could, I am sure, have made his mark in any form of comedy he liked—high or low. But he was a remote and aloof man, and his work and approach were far too subtle for some of the rougher music-halls. He was, in fact, a law unto himself, and certainly no respector of persons. He is a brilliant lecturer and writer, a number one expert on heraldry, and has studied law. In his private life, he is a strict church-going Anglo-Catholic, but in his approach to variety he was a real Non-conformist, going his own way and disdainfully indifferent to either audience or managerial reaction. At times he could devastate an audience, and he made, possibly, the greatest success any single turn comedian has ever made at a Royal Variety Performance, at the London Palladium on 22 May 1930.

Gillie now lives in retirement at Bournemouth, but every now and then a letter or an article of his in *The Times*, or some other National, reminds us that Gillie still speaks to us in English!

There are a distinguished few among the variety profession who can claim to have become legends in their own lifetime, and my old friend Albert Whelan was undoubtedly one of these. It is only a short while since his death and I still can't realize that Albert won't be there when I go to my Water Rats Lodge meetings, because, in spite of the illness that he had in his latter years culminating finally in the loss of his leg, nothing stopped him from either coming to Lodge or appearing before the public.

Many great stars are woven into our music-hall tapestry, and Albert Whelan's name looms large on this magical brocade. He came to England from Australia to bring a new and cultured approach with a variety act that was an adornment where adornment was much needed, and, for over fifty years, he remained a star in his own right, meeting the changing conditions of entertainment with a resilience and an optimism that was only equalled by the fortitude and guts with which he faced the removal of his leg. A veteran of over fourscore years, he made a mockery of age, simply because he was young in heart and youthful in outlook and adhered to his own immaculate standards.

In these days, when signature tunes are so common that they have almost lost their individuality, it is interesting to recall that Albert's famous signature tune—"The Jolly Brothers" (or in German, "Lustige Brüder")—which he whistled on his entrance and again on his exit, was the first. I can picture him now, coming through that centre opening, immaculate in silk hat, evening coat, white muffler, and gloves, lazily whistling this tune—and it was no ordinary whistle—as he gracefully removed his garments, laid them

down, and then began his act. In his early days he would
often start his act on his own at the piano with songs like
"The Preacher and the Bear," or that delicious little song
monologue about the "Three Trees" which were "There—
There—and THERE."

Albert could be said to have been almost a complete contrast to the current stars of that period, because, whilst they
always attacked when they commenced an act, Albert appeared
to amble on and laze his way, with complete nonchalance, into
his work, and, when it was done, the tall, lean figure, would
gracefully bow, and then—just as lazily—pick up his coat, his
muffler, his hat, and his gloves, whilst he whistled that delightful signature tune once more—and then, on its last notes,
he would gently stroll out of the scene.

Although an Australian, he had not the slightest trace of
an Australian accent, and here again was a man always willing
to help a brother artist. I appeared in many variety shows with
him, and was flattered that he took a great interest in my
work, and particularly, in my material. His advice was invaluable to me on countless occasions. And Albert had a
way of giving advice without any pomposity, or the smug
"I-know-it-all" attitude that some of the big stars adopted.
He could almost make you feel you had thought of what he
had told you yourself. Many years ago, he said to me: "Clarkie
—always remember that though what you do may please the
public at the time, the most important thing is the impression
you leave behind." How right he was—and how well he
lived up to this precept.

He was a Past King Rat of the Grand Order of Water Rats,
and we in the Order always regarded him as one of our
Elder Statesmen. His tremendous resilience was never more
evidenced than when, nearing his eighties, he had to have his
leg off, and in spite of what the doctors predicted he was up
and about and using his false leg months before they said he
would be able to. I shall always be conscious of the great
honour that befell Olive and myself and our show *Twinkle*

when, after a brief convalescence at Bognor, he was able to
visit my show at Worthing and make his first public appearance after his operation.

A few years before he died the Water Rats decided to present
an all-star testimonial show in his honour on a Sunday night
at the Victoria Palace. I was fortunate enough to be the
reigning King Rat and to have the privilege of starting the
evening off with a prologue that I had specially written as a
tribute to this great artist and much respected man; and the
number and quality of the artists who turned up for this performance, is indicative of the affection in which Albert was
held by us all. I would like now to recall this tribute—and
here it is . . .

> As King Rat of this Order, on behalf of all my Court,
> I thank you for your presence, and your generous support,
> In helping us, the Water Rats, to pay the homage due
> To someone whom we love a lot—and we know you love him,
>   too.
> From Australia, sixty years ago, he landed in these parts,
> And, in a trice, had whistled into everybody's hearts.
> It doesn't come to everyone, no matter who you are,
> To arrive here as a stranger, and at once become a star.
> For sixty years, this ageless man has been just that—what's
>   more
> At eighty odd, he looks much like he did at twenty-four.
> The music-halls, when Albert came, were very much alive
> With vivid personalities, vitality and drive.
> Dan Leno, Arthur Roberts' earthy humour, ripe and rich,
> Marie Lloyd, Harry Lauder, Vesta Tilley, Little Tich
> 'Midst the Robeys and the Strattons and the Dunvilles and the
>   Tates
> Albert took his place at once—a great among the greats.
> And probably those former stars—wherever they may be,
> Are joining us tonight for Albert's Diamond Jubilee.
> This wonder from down under's always been a shining light
> Both on the stage, and off it, too—and that is why, tonight
> The cream of our profession have gathered like a clan

To pay our loving tribute to a trouper and a man.
And when he had his leg off, never once did he complain,
And at his age, with splendid guts, he's learned to walk again.
And when this show is over, you'll be very proud to say
You really did a splendid job, this memorable day,
In helping us, the Water Rats, to properly acclaim
A legend in his lifetime—Albert Whelan is the name!

After this came a programme which, for quality and quantity, has seldom, if ever, been equalled. Dickie Henderson, Audrey Jeans, Yana, Wilfred Pickles, Charlie Chester, Anne Shelton, Bud Flanagan and Chesney Allen, Max Jaffa—with Jack Byfield and Reginald Kilby—Max Bygraves, Ben Warriss, Ted Ray, Evelyn Laye, Tommy Trinder, The Three Monarchs, The Luton Girls' Choir, Frankie Vaughan, and Sidney Jerome and his Orchestra. This will give you some idea of what his brothers and sisters in the profession thought of him!

CHAPTER XII

A JOLLY LOT OF FELLOWS

"A JOLLY lot of fellows are the Water Rats" is the final line of the Anthem used by the Grand Order of Water Rats in their ceremonies and meetings, and it is as apt a description as any of as jolly a lot of fellows as one could find in any community. Founded in 1889, at the Magpie Hotel in Sunbury-on-Thames, it has through the years had a tremendous influence on the social and material betterment of the variety profession. Its founder and inspiration was the lovable Joe Elvin, the cockney comedian, who in company with Wal Pink, Jack Lotto, Fred and Joe Griffiths, Arthur Forrest, Barney Armstrong, Tom Brantford, George Fairburn, and George Harris took a river trip one Sunday afternoon to Sunbury, and ended up with a convivial dinner at the Magpie Hotel. Good food, good wine, and good comradeship breed good and kindly thoughts, and, this spirit prevailing, the Grand Order of Water Rats was conceived. I don't suppose those original founders ever envisaged the day when the Water Rats Anthem would be heard on radio and the Water Rats themselves seen doing television shows, but if their good and kindly spirits are aware of our modern activities in this way I am sure they are very proud.

"Why are we called the Water Rats?" people often ask, and my chief authority, of course, comes from our late, much beloved and respected preceptor, Fred Russell, who though not an original member of the fraternity was very soon to be closely associated with it. There are many ideas about the origin of the name, but, roughly speaking, it came from a racing pony. Joe Elvin, Jack Lotto and James Finney had always been interested in racing. James Finney, who was a top-liner at that time, with his diving displays, was fulfilling an engagement at the Empire in South Shields—then under the control of the redoubtable Dick Thornton who owned a racing pony called "The Magpie." Finney reported this to his pals, Joe and Jack, and, in short, the pony was brought to London where these three formed a sort of co-operative syndicate with Mr. Thornton and the pony was entered for races, and was very successful.

One day, the story goes, Joe Elvin was driving the pony home in a heavy rainstorm. The animal was absolutely soaked, and presented a drenched, dejected appearance. In the Brixton Road a bus driver shouted to Elvin " 'Allo there, Joe, old cock. What the hell have you got there?" "A trotter," replied Joe. "Trotter, me arse," said the bus driver. "It looks more like a water rat!" There was naturally a pull-up at the local, and the pony was duly christened "The Water Rat." And, at that dinner at the Magpie Hotel, when the fraternity was first formed the boys called it "Pals of the Water Rat," which subsequently became "The Select Order of Water Rats" and finally "The Grand Order of Water Rats." Its motto and objects were "philanthropy, conviviality, and social intercourse." Wal Pink, a brilliant author of his time, wrote the original ritual, which, in substance, is still in use to this very day.

Most of the stars, past and present, have been and are members of the Order—and not only stars of our own country but of many others. But let me here say that the Order is not restricted to stars; any member of the profession and its allied interests can apply for membership, and, if fulfilling the necessary qualifications, will be admitted. Today, the Order is stronger than ever, and, moving with the times, embraces men from all fields of entertainment. However, it isn't easy to become a Water Rat, and membership is a hall-mark of the esteem in which one is held by one's fellows, and demands first-class qualities of character.

Since those early days the face of entertainment has changed rapidly. Two world wars have almost obliterated the gracious and leisurely ease that the founders of the Water Rats enjoyed. Nevertheless, the Order's objects are still the same—good comradeship, tolerance, justice, and, above all, generosity; and their benevolence extends not only to their own Brothers in the Order who are in need, but to countless other charities that have called upon them from time to time—and these calls are increasing every day.

Some thirty years ago we added a new page to our history by admitting prominent people and lovers of our profession as Companions to the Order, and their interest and benevolence have been wonderful. By their aid, too, we have been able to embrace schemes which have not only brought grist to many charity mills, but have enhanced our prestige in no small measure.

Our first Companion was the late Sir Noel Curtis-Bennett, and he and his lovely and gracious wife were enthusiastic and eager supporters of the variety profession in general—and of the G.O.W.R. in particular. I recall many occasions when Sir Noel would drive from his lovely Sussex home to theatres and music-halls where he knew certain Water Rats were appearing. He took a joyous interest in all our doings and it was he who undoubtedly blazed the trail of illustrious people who are now our Companions. We mourn him, as we mourn Sir Louis Stirling. Sir Louis was another early Companion, and nothing gave him greater joy than to join us in Lodge on a Sunday night.

Joseph Fenston, or Joe as he was known to us all, died only recently, in fact, soon after he became a Companion; and how he revelled in his Companionship. He was another who loved to come to Lodge and be among the "boys," and, of course, he had on many occasions been closely associated with the theatre and sponsored several enterprises.

It was one of the greatest ambitions of Hannen Swaffer to join our Order, and the night he was initiated he really let himself go in a nostalgic speech lasting nearly an hour! He, too, was realizing a long-cherished wish. Hannen was a strange man—a mixture of mystic, hermit, and showman. Known as "The Pope of Fleet Street," he was a most ardent spiritualist. In his heyday he was dogmatic, and, when he pursued any particular obsession, he could be vitriolic. But, unlike some of the younger journalists of today who write about entertainment, he had a vast knowledge of the subject, and, whilst it is my belief that a critic primarily tries to sell himself rather than the wares he is plugging, Swaffer's criticisms were at least backed by a tremendous insight and know-how of the machinery of the theatre and the music-hall. He would, I am sure, have been the first to admit that he was an exhibitionist. Nightly, he would sit in the same seat in the Savoy Lounge, cigarette drooping from those tight lips, ash all over his flowing tie and lapels. Nothing gave him greater joy than the time when he was slapped by an actress after he had given rather a devastating criticism of her work! He basked in the great publicity this brought!

He was not to be our Companion for long, and his passing means that we have lost some very rich moments in Lodge.

Yes, indeed, we are grateful for our Companions—an impressive list, who, at the time of writing, are—

His Royal Highness, Prince Philip, Duke of Edinburgh,
    K.G., K.T.

The Rt. Hon. Viscount Alexander of Hillsborough, P.C.G.H.

Sir Alan P. Herbert

W. E. Butlin, Esq., M.B.E.

Val Parnell, Esq.

Jack Hylton, Esq.

Tom Arnold, Esq.

E. Barry Webber, Esq.

Dr. A. P. Magonet

Lord Douglas of Kirtleside

J. Rosser Chinn, Esq.
W. James Moore, Esq., J.P.
Jack Jay, Esq.
Leslie A. Macdonnel, Esq., O.B.E.
Eric Miller, Esq.
Bernard Delfont, Esq.
F. W. Pontin, Esq.
William Foux, Esq.—who is also our Hon. Solicitor,
    and,
Andrew Neatrour, Esq.—our indefatigable Public Relations
    bloke.
The Rt. Hon. Viscount Tenby, P.C., T.D., J.P.
Lt.-Col. A. Basil Brown, T.D.
Larry Webb.

I wonder what dear Joe Elvin would think if he could see us today? How he would have revelled in our Greyhound Meetings at Harringay; how those expressive eyes would have goggled when His Royal Highness, Prince Philip, Duke of Edinburgh, was installed as a Companion at the Mayfair Hotel. I can hear him now saying—"Cor blimey—what a turn-up for the book!"

CHAPTER XIII

TWO MEMORABLE NIGHTS

Since the Grand Order of Water Rats was founded there have naturally been many notable and memorable occasions, and it would not be possible here to recall all—or even a few—of those with which I have been associated; and so I will content myself by telling you about just two of them.

The first took place on 1 November 1931, when Charlie Chaplin was initiated into our Order. Our headquarters were then in Old Compton Street, and every Water Rat who could be there was there—and not only that, but was there at the appointed time! I must here explain that our ceremonies of initiation take place at a given time and that punctuality is observed, and in any case, even if there should be a slight delay in starting owing to prior business, the initiate himself is always there on time, waiting with his sponsors to be called to what he undoubtedly regards as an ordeal.

We knew, of course, that Chaplin was on a fleeting visit to London, but Charlie Austin, who was his sponsor and a great personal friend, had guaranteed to have him there on time. Well, the appointed time arrived—but there was no Charlie Chaplin. Instead, there came a phone call from Charlie Austin telling us not to worry, he wouldn't be long. So we settled down to chat and take refreshment. I can see that room now. Among those present were Georgie Wood— who, incidentally, was not only Chaplin's seconder but who had been a very close associate, Harry Tate and his son

Ronnie—and Ronnie still vividly recalls that evening with his characteristic chuckle over lots of things that happened, Stanley Damerell, Hal Jones, Dave O'Toole, Jimmy Nervo, Freddie Malcolm, Dave O'Gorman, Dusty Rhodes, Bud Flanagan, Talbot O'Farrell, Albert Egbert, Will Fyffe, Jack Hylton, Con Kenna, Douglas Wakefield, G. S. Melvin, Norman Long, and George Jackley—to name but a few from a packed assembly. I sat quietly with Arthur Astor—or, as he was known, A. C. Astor, "the globe-trotting ventriloquist." Arthur was a great friend of mine, and we had shared many happy occasions together. Apart from being one of the first people to introduce novelty into the ventriloquial art he had an excellent flair for writing articles, and his "Just Jottings," which were a weekly feature of *The Stage* for some time were typical of his outlook, his philosophy, and his intelligence, and we were both vastly entertained by the various reactions to what some wag of these days would have undoubtedly called "Waiting for Godot"—and there was, I assure you, a lot to amuse us!

An hour passed by—and still no Chaplin. There were murmurings from some of the Rats, and human nature being what it is some of the bigger names got rather annoyed. There were remarks such as "Why should we have to wait? We are the Grand Order of Water Rats, initiates don't keep *us* waiting," and so on. Another well-known star said: "Well, I'm not waiting much longer—another ten minutes, and I'm off." Nevertheless, many ten minutes went by, and he was still there. At the end of another hour things were getting quite restless. Poor Charlie Austin must have been in a terrible state because he phoned again and begged us not to break up. There had been a hitch, but Chaplin was definitely coming, and he would bring him. The murmurings grew louder and louder, and the aforementioned star, who had been going in ten minutes, announced that this delay was an insult to the Water Rats—Chaplin or no Chaplin; and that, as far as he was concerned, it was the finish and he was off. And, with that, he went out—but only to the cloak-room!

Then came yet another phone call; Chaplin was definitely on his way, but, even then, he was being mobbed by crowds outside the Ritz Hotel. Eventually, after a delay of nearly three hours, in came Charlie Austin with the great Charlie Chaplin.

The arrival of the great little clown produced an amazing contrast in the atmosphere and mood of the meeting, and it really was remarkable and amusing to watch some of those who had been loudest in their complaints at the delay change their tone at once and became almost sycophantic in the warmth of their welcome and their adulation with remarks like "How are you, Charlie boy?" or, a veteran Water Rat would say to a younger one, "I was on the bill many times with him when he was with Fred Karno," or, perhaps pityingly, "Yes—you wouldn't know him when he was with the 'Lancashire Lads'."

We have always claimed in the Water Rats—and rightly so —that it is a great honour to become a Rat, but we would not be truthful if we didn't admit that on this particular night we were, perhaps, more conscious of the honour being conferred on us by the world's greatest comedian. I don't think anyone present will ever forget Charlie Chaplin's poise and dignity during the ceremony. Will Hay was the King Rat that particular year—truly one of the best we have ever had—and, after the making, Will graciously handed over to Charlie Austin, and it was nearly midnight when Charlie Chaplin at last became a Water Rat.

Those present will never forget the wonderful one-man performance he gave us afterwards; it was his pet party piece —"Carlos, the Bullfighter"—just a perfect observance in mime. It was in the early hours of the morning when we finished, buses having been missed and train connections to the provinces lost, but it didn't seem to matter; everything in the garden, which, earlier on had revealed quite a lot of irritation and some discord, turned out to be lovely and harmonious, and quite a number of us went off with Chaplin to Charlie Austin's flat in Ridgmount Gardens, to listen to the two Charlies competing in memories of the days of "Casey's Court."

Red-letter days for the Rats are not as frequent as they used to be, for many reasons—not the least of which must be the changing face of our profession. But Sunday 10 September 1961 was a real red-letter day for us—one might almost say a tri-coloured day—for that was the Sunday when Maurice Chevalier came to Lodge. He had been over here making a film, and, of course, received the normal summons, which all Rats receive as a matter of course, but we had to thank Cardew Robinson—known to many readers for his famous "Cardew, the Cad of the School" broadcasts—for making sure he came; and, incidentally, what an indefatigable Rat Cardew Robinson is—always scheming, planning, and doing for us.

You can imagine what a thrill it must have been for our King Rat in that year—Ben Warriss—to welcome this great man back. As one would expect from a good showman, Ben welcomed others first, and kept the "top-of-the-bill," so to speak, until the last. This, of course, was no disrespect to the others, whatever their status, but simply in the showman traditions of our profession. As I have mentioned before, there is no question of lesser fry in the Rats; once in Lodge, a Rat is a Rat—

> We do not ask from whence you came,
> Or whether great or small your name,
> Your nationality and fame
> When once a Rat—are all the same.

So reads part of our ritual in our initiation ceremony. But in any case, most people are snobs at heart—inverted or otherwise—and it was fitting and right on this occasion, that billing order was reserved.

Big welcomes were given first to two Rats whom we hadn't

seen for some time—Bobby May and Vic Marlowe. And then came the great moment—"Welcome back to Rat Maurice Chevalier" . . . and he was, of course, given a standing ovation. Up he got, this great Gaelic charmer, possibly the most famous of all French artists since Sarah Bernhardt. So part and parcel of the international scene in entertainment has he become that there are times when I don't look upon him as a Frenchman; he seems to belong to us all. There he stood white hair, pink complexion, the protruding lower lip, the flashing smile, and the pearly teeth—teeth that make a toothpaste advertisement look dirty—and for twenty minutes or more he told us, as only he could, of his early days when he first came here in 1905, and took a small room in Little Newport Street where he could see the big stars entering and leaving the stage door of the London Hippodrome. "Nevaire deed I think that I would one day be on the 'Ippodrome stage, doing my one-man show, as a beeg star." He then told us how much he owed to the British music-hall artists he had met—and in particular he cited "Georges Robee, 'Arry Tate, Maree Lloyd—and that great arteest, Wilkee Bard. I learnt such a lot from them, and I go back to Paris and what I 'ave learnt I remember and use with my own talent, and soon, thanks to what you call am-al-ga-mation, I am a star, and I owe it seventee-five per cent to Briteesh music-'all arteests."

This, and a lot more, in his engaging, not-so-broken English, was a great treat for us all; thank heaven indeed, for artists like Maurice Chevalier!

Past King Rat Georgie Wood replied, as usual, brilliantly, and his reference to a slip in the programme when he went to see Chevalier's one-man-show at the Hippodrome, and his fear that it might be announcing the great Maurice's inability to appear, and that the deputy would be a certain sturdy British music-hall artist, brought the biggest laugh of the evening!

I have selected these two particular occasions as memorable, because they concern two world-famous and international

18.—Tommy Steele: proving that the youngsters can be more than Pop Guitar players.

19.—Her Majesty the Queen visits Butlin's Pwllheli Camp and is escorted by Billy Butlin, O.B.E., with (*in the background*) his Director of Entertainments, Lieut.-Col. Basil Brown, T.D.

stars; two people who have become something more in the public eye than merely entertainers; in the same way that Sir Winston Churchill is loved by all—not because he is a politician, and not only because he was a great Prime Minister, but because as Winston or Winnie—whichever you like—he became our idol. There have been—and will be—many others.

CHAPTER XIV

ROYAL OCCASIONS

HIS Royal Highness, Prince Philip, Duke of Edinburgh has honoured the Grand Order of Water Rats by becoming a Companion of the Order. Undoubtedly the way was paved for this important occasion when the Order arranged a Midnight Matinée at the Victoria Palace on 9 December 1957— the proceeds of which we had agreed to devote to His Royal Highness's favourite charity—The London Federation of Boys' Clubs. And I was indeed fortunate that this event occurred the day after I had been installed as King Rat of the Order, and that I had the privilege of doing the particular honours on behalf of the Order that evening, and being a sort of "Cicerone" to the Prince.

At a quarter to twelve the Duke and his equerry arrived at the doors of the theatre. He was met by Jack Hylton and myself, and my first job was to present the beautiful Duchess of Argyll, Chairman of the Committee organizing the event. This over, I escorted the Duke to meet a line-up of Past Kings including Bud Flanagan, Ben Warriss, Cyril Dowler, Charlie Chester, Albert Whelan, George Elrick, George Doonan, Dave O'Gorman, and Georgie Wood. I finally conducted the Prince to his box.

The programme was a gigantic one and I cannot mention all who took part, but it was far more representative of the British music-hall than the usual Royal Performance. Among the many artists appearing were Gracie Fields, David Nixon,

Peter Cavanagh, Eddie Calvert, Jon Pertwee, Jewell and
Warriss, Nadia Nerina, Tommy Trinder, Jimmy Wheeler,
Frankie Vaughan, Alfred Marks, Arthur Askey, Max Bygraves,
Charlie Chester, Alma Cogan, Tommy Cooper, Nervo and
Knox, Naughton and Gold, Bobby Howes, Vera Lynn, Vic
Oliver, Wilfred Pickles, Sandy Powell, Harry Secombe,
Anne Shelton, Jack Train, Dickie Valentine, Max Wall,
Albert Whelan, Yana, The Television Toppers, and The
Tiller Girls.

During the interval the Duke said that he would like to
see the great speedboat ace, Donald Campbell, who had been
watching the show—so he was brought in. Then came David
Nixon, who presented the Prince with two large boxes of
conjuring tricks for Prince Charles and Princess Anne.

It is surprising how Prince Philip always seems to know
about the work and the jobs of the people he is talking to
whatever their occupation, and his vivid outlook and sense of
humour on these occasions is a wonderful help to anyone like
myself, who feels the awe and responsibility of looking after
royalty at such events as this.

After the show it was my job to take the Duke backstage
and introduce him to the cast, and as I escorted him along the
line, he had something appropriate to say to everybody he
was introduced to, and one could not help but marvel at his
wonderful observation. This had been particularly evidenced
earlier on when he very carefully examined my King Rat's
Collar, on which are emblazoned the names of all the Past
King Rats on little brass plates.

Yes, it was a great night in every way; great entertainment, less formal than the usual Royal Performances, and
relaxed in atmosphere throughout; and for this, we rightly
have to thank the gracious, knowledgeable and—may I
respectfully say—matey atmosphere radiated by Prince Philip
himself.

The next royal occasion for the Water Rats, was when the
Duke was installed as a Companion of the Order. This was

at a specially arranged luncheon at the Mayfair Hotel on 10 March 1960. In that particular year I was Preceptor of the Order; I should explain here that the Preceptor is responsible for the carrying out of the rules, the procedure, and the main part of the Initiation and Installation ceremonies. I had the honour of writing a special Installation ceremony for His Royal Highness, and proud of this as I was I realized afterwards that because of it and because of its formality, its dignity, and its seriousness, I was not able to be part of the fun and the jokes which other Officers of the Order were able to indulge in, and watching the ceremony afterwards on television I saw myself striking the only sombre and serious note in the whole affair. Still, somebody had to do it, and it was the Preceptor's job.

Apart from that it was indeed a gay occasion, and how could it be otherwise with such brilliantly witty clowns as Tommy Trinder, Ted Ray, and Bud Flanagan? Tommy quipped about not being able to land his helicopter in the gardens of Buckingham Palace; Bud Flanagan, a particular favourite of the Duke's, pulled several cracks; and Ted Ray was at his superb best, and his shafts about the new baby, Prince Andrew, were just simply rays of Ted's best sunshine. He presented the Duke with a teddy-bear for the newly born Prince. But the professional funsters and their jokes were well matched by Prince Philip himself. When our Trustee, Nat Mills, handed him the cheque for the Playing Fields Association, examining it carefully the Prince looked at his watch and quipped "It's only just two o'clock, I think I'll get this in the bank right away."

Prior to the luncheon Prince Philip again showed his uncanny memory as he came down the ranks of the Past King Rats and other Officers of the Order asking potent questions and recalling incidents and faces that he had met at that earlier function at the Victoria Palace; and again, when Bud Flanagan took him round the Rats' Museum, which is a collection of relics and trade-marks of some of our former greats—such as Little Tich's boots, Fred Russell's ventriloquial figure "Coster Joe," Cruikshank's banjo, and so on.

The luncheon and the ceremony were timed to finish at half-past two, and at that time His Royal Highness's Detective, Mr. Kelley, appeared very anxious to get him away to whatever other appointment he might have had, but the Duke was having none of it. He stayed long after half-past two, and then seemed reluctant to leave us. It was a great day for the Order. One could not help but notice that Rats who had not been to Lodge for years managed to get to this particular function, and the capacity of the Mayfair Ballroom was taxed to its utmost. As Jack Hylton pinned the emblem of our Order—a golden Water Rat—in the Duke's lapel, my mind wandered into the past and I wished that the original founders could look in on us and share in the pride and the fun of this great royal occasion.

I have already mentioned that my initial royal experience was the Royal Performance at the Coliseum on 1 March 1928. I arrived from Birmingham for rehearsal at the theatre on the morning of the performance, and oh dear, what a time of tension it was! The great Alfred Dove was the Coliseum's musical director—and a very good one, but not noted for his patience. By the time the acts had been vetted and screened, and vetted and screened again, all of us, with the possible exception of Will Hay, were in a real state of nerves. Will Hay was a seasoned royal performer by that time, whereas the others on the programme were first timers. The cast included Larry Kemble, a quaint little Scottish trick cyclist; Stanelli and Douglas, with their fiddle fanatics; A. C. Astor, the ventriloquist; Lilian Burgess, a lovely soprano; Noni, the French clown (often known as the poor man's Grock!); Gracie Fields; Jack Hylton's Band; Victor André; Anton Dolin; The Victoria Palace Girls; and myself.

When I got into the theatre that night there was a suppressed air of excitement, irritability, and strain about everything and everybody. The Coliseum staff, under the admirable

Mr. Crocker, were always a highly specialized and almost autocratic body of men, all wearing Plimsolls, to deaden backstage noise, and dressed in immaculate overalls. I have mentioned before that seasoned music-hall performers will tell you that they never felt they were in a music-hall when they were at the Coliseum; it was more like a cathedral, and yet it was the showplace of the world at the time.

Presently there was a hush, a roll of drums, a fanfare, and the National Anthem, and we could hear the rustle of dresses and the snapping back of tip-up seats as the audience rose in one body and King George V and Queen Mary, accompanied by equerries and ladies-in-waiting, entered the royal box. Some of the artists tried to peep through the curtain to have a look, but they were sharply ordered away by the stern Mr. Crocker.

The show began. I wasn't on until the second half; I simply couldn't hang around, so I went out to the stage door. There I met a well-known agent. "Hullo, Clarkie," he said, "you ought to be inside." "No," I replied, "I'm not on until the second half, and I feel I must get some fresh air." "Feeling a bit jumpy?" he asked. "I certainly am," I replied. "How long have you got before you're on?" "Oh, at least an hour and a half." "Right," he said, "come on down to the club and have a game of snooker." And, to my ultimate sorrow, I did. Snooker usually relaxes me, but it didn't that night; and after the game, the friendly agent said: "Take my tip, Clarkie—have a good stiff whisky, it will steady you." And I foolishly took his advice. He came back with me to the theatre, and into the dressing-room, while I got ready for my act. True it was only one whisky he had given me, but I think it must have been a treble, and I was not in the habit of taking a drink before my work.

The warning buzzer rang on the intercom in my dressing-room, and a staccato voice said: "Mr. Rose, you're on in five minutes." Down I went from my room, through the labyrinth of corridors, and reached the side of the stage. The whisky hadn't steadied me; it had gone to my head and destroyed my perspective. I heard my introductory music coming, as it were, from a distance, and I walked on for my first song in a kind of trance. I completed it, and left the stage to make my change into a bustle to sing "Girls of the Old Brigade." My first song had received polite applause— but only polite, and I felt I had flopped. Back I went in my bustle, and, what with the whisky and the mixed-up feelings of not doing well after the first verse and chorus, I slipped down the highly polished slope leading to the footlights; my bustle went up in the air to disclose my red bloomers! It was a godsend, because Queen Mary was seen to rock backwards and forwards with laughter, and, luckily for me, at that moment the Press took a flashlight photograph of the royal box, which appeared in many of the national newspapers the next day. From then on all was easy and I couldn't do wrong, but it was the first—and last—time that I have ever taken a stimulant before a show!

Next day a leading "daily" commented: "King George seemed to know all about the references to 'laying the lino on the floor,' in the topical song Mr. Clarkson Rose sang first, but Queen Mary was more amused with his delicious burlesque of a Victorian dame, and the little trip he did, displaying voluminous underclothing, caused roars of laughter, led by Her Majesty." What a bit of unexpected luck!

Most artists will tell you that Royal Performances are abnormal affairs; possible exceptions are Bud Flanagan and the Crazy Gang, who have done so many that they could almost claim to have had a career of them. But they are not normal shows in any respect. The audience, in the main, have come because it is a Royal Performance, and it is most difficult to entertain them because they have one eye focused on the Royal Box all the time to see if royalty are approving or not. It's a sort of divided focus, and very difficult to deal with. Many well-known stars have flopped under the weight of the occasion, including the brilliant Danny Kaye.

Finally, I want to tell you about one of the most extraordinary royal occasions I have ever experienced. It was the Royal Automobile Club twenty-fifth anniversary celebrations at the Covent Garden Opera House, which was attended by the present Duke of Windsor—then Prince of Wales. This was in 1931, and was really more in the nature of a Command Performance than the annual Royal Variety Performance, previously known as the Royal *Command* Variety Performance, in which the artists are picked, in the main, by the management who control the theatre, whereas the real Command Performances are those in which the artists are bidden to go to Windsor, or some other royal residence, by the Buckingham Palace authorities themselves. In this Covent Garden affair the artists had been chosen by the Prince of Wales himself and the R.A.C. management in conjunction with various variety big-wigs. The show did not go on until ten-thirty at night, being preceded by a huge banquet on the stage, in full view of the audience!

It was a wonderful programme, and certainly more carefree than most royal occasions. I was honoured to be included, with such names as Harry Tate, Nellie Wallace, Ella Shields, Albert Whelan, Clarice Mayne, Nelson Keys, Du Calion, Tom Clare, Georgie Wood, and Will Hay; and in addition to the full programme, several acts had been called from the various London halls to stand by as deputies in case of any late arrivals among the chosen artists—many of whom were appearing at various suburban music-halls. One well-known man-and-wife double act were elated at being chosen, and as the show went on and they were not needed they got very irritated, and kept going to the stage manager and asking "When are we on?" Finally, the stage manager said: "You're on in about ten minutes." Just then a message came from the front of the house to say that the Prince of Wales was leaving early, and that he wished to see two of his favourite acts before he went—those acts being Nelson Keys in a sketch with Irene Russell, and Harry Tate and his famous "Motoring" sketch. The double act standing by heard this message and the hurried directions given to the stage staff to get the various settings ready for these two acts. "You said we were on in ten minutes," said the irate male partner to the stage manager. "I'm awfully sorry, Mister. . . . It can't be helped, the Prince of Wales is leaving shortly, and wishes to see Mr. Tate's and Mr. Key's acts before he goes, and we are getting ready for them." "Well, we can go on now, whilst you are getting ready—I know he'd like our act." "That's as maybe, but you can't go on now; you require a full set, and so does Mr. Keys, so I am sending Mr. Clarkson Rose on in a front-cloth, while we set behind," and on I went!

When I came off the double act were still at the side of the stage—and really in a rage. "We've been here all night, Clarkie, standing by, and now the Prince of Wales is going, and won't see us." However, he was slightly compensated when he received—as we all did—an evening dress cigarette case, engraved with the Royal Coat of Arms; the ladies had a silver powder-box. Artists don't receive anything for ordinary Royal Performances, and it was nice to have these excellent souvenirs.

And, furthermore, there was something else which we don't normally get at royal shows—a sumptuous running buffet backstage, quite one of the richest and most heavily laden I have ever seen. The R.A.C., of course, is noted for its first-class food and catering, and this buffet was in the charge of liveried, be-wigged and powdered footmen. Lobsters, prawns, salmon, trout, chickens, quails, hams, tongues, galantines—sandwiches of every type, and sweetmeats were there in profusion—and as for liquor there was enough to make a Hogmanay night in Glasgow look like a temperance meeting! Some of our fraternity are abstemious on these occasions, others are not, and one of the latter was that very splendid artist, Du Calion, known as "The Loquacious Laddie on the Tottering Ladder," and, in passing, let me say that "Duke"—as he was known to us all—was one of the most sought-after artists of his day and age, and was really brilliant. He would climb on to his tall ladder unaided, but, by his deft balancing, make it look almost fixed, and when he reached the top an attractive assistant would come on and hand him up a mando-lin, and he would then play his tune and patter jokingly in an ad lib. manner. He was quite uninhibited and quite irreverent, and having daringly described the physical charms of his delightful assistant he would discourse pungently on various topics. He could even disturb the somnolence of a London Coliseum matinée audience. Moreover, he was no respecter of persons, and I remember one occasion when finding lack of audience reaction he addressed the audience with Sir Oswald Stoll sitting in his box, and complained about his own spot on the programme and the dullness of the audience!

But to get back to the buffet. When the show was over, Duke and I, who were sharing a dressing-room, went down to take refreshment. It was very late, and gradually, as some of the artists and some odd visitors began to leave, I saw Duke in whispered consultation with one of the footmen— and this particular chap had, I think, taken full advantage of the ample supply of liquor! Suddenly Duke disappeared then returned with a suitcase, and, to my consternation, he pro-ceeded to fill it up with delicacies from the buffet! "Duke," I protested, "you can't do that." "Why not?" he replied, "it's provided for us—and there's a lot left!" I remonstrated with him, but to no avail, and having filled his suitcase he calmly stood at the buffet and started eating! He lived at Golders Green, and so did I so he promised me a lift home. When he had finished his "eats," he calmly said: "Thanks very much boys—goodnight. Come on, Clarkie." And picking up his suitcase he led the way to his car!

CHAPTER XV

THREE-COURSE SUPPER—ONE AND SIX!

It's hardly believable, is it? Eighteen pence for a three-course supper. But this, I assure you, was not unusual. I am quoting from an advertisement in the programme of the Empire Theatre, Leicester Square, on 24 June 1901. The restaurant in question was Pinoli's—a favourite rendezvous of Bohemian London until about twenty-five years ago. Their advertisement read—

A Special 1/6 Supper
Is served from 9 p.m. to 12.15 p.m.
consisting of
SOUP, FISH, ENTREE or POULTRY, VEGETABLES, ICE, CHEESE

Take it from me—the food was ample and very good. If you think that this is cheap—and it *is* cheap, by any standards—what about this, which was advertised in the programme of the Palace Theatre, Shaftesbury Avenue, on 16 November 1899 by "The Hotel et Restaurant Brice, *Maison Française*," which was in Old Compton Street. They not only offered you a *table d'hote* at one shilling and sixpence, but also a very special more expensive one at two shillings and sixpence, which, furthermore, included the following: "N.B. This Hotel supplies a *table d'hote* dinner at 2/6, including wine and coffee." In these days, when it is wise to get an estimate before ordering, it makes you think, doesn't it? In fact, all the advertisements in these beautiful programmes conjure up the luxurious and relaxed atmosphere of a nation whose flag flew over a quarter of the world at that time—a time when the golden sovereign was really worth twenty shillings in the pound, and the prices, compared with present-day standards, were astounding. For example, Mr. Dunn advertised his famous bowler hats at three shillings and ninepence, and emphasized that they were "all one price." You could get a bottle of James Buchanan's Whisky, for three shillings and sixpence! But, as an uncle once remarked to me, that was dear, because you could get a very good Glenlivet for three shillings, at so-and-so's off-licence!

Another advertisement told us that "A perfect and graceful figure is assured to every lady wearing the H.S. Corsets." The illustration of this garment looks rather like armour, but, nevertheless, that is what they wore. A similar advertisement for "Y.C. Corsets"—sub-titled, the "Patti"—gives the prices as two and elevenpence halfpenny to twenty-one shillings! Madame Patti, of course, was the most famous prima donna of the day.

In a programme of the Alhambra Theatre, Leicester Square, dated the week commencing 14 February 1898, we are told that when we are turning grey we can darken the hair with "Condy's Fluid"—and this would cost you a shilling a bottle! To preserve our complexions we are further urged to buy "Dr. Duncan's Mouilla Liquid Soap," which is backed by "Testimonials from numbers of the Nobility, Ladies, Gentry, and Medical Profession, which accompany each bottle." This bottle would have cost you a shilling, or, if you wanted to be extravagant and have a double size—one shilling and sixpence! In an Empire Theatre, Leicester Square programme, for 24 June 1901, the same firm had a full-page advertisement which read as follows: "A Woman Is As Old As She Looks," and it goes on to tell one "How to keep Young," urging you again to buy "Mouilla," which, according to this particular advertisement, tells you that it "possesses unrivalled powers for rendering the skin smooth and soft, and its constant use

will be a sure safe-guard against the formation of wrinkles."
Price—a shilling a bottle!

Having dealt with some of the advertisements, let us turn
to the entertainment provided, and take a peep at the programme presented at the Oxford music-hall during the week
ending 29 June 1895. It was opened by a big overture called
"Albion," followed by Mr. Horace Mills—Comic Vocalist;
many will probably still remember this excellent comedy actor
who later became one of the most famous pantomime dames
we have ever had—in some ways, more like Dan Leno than
anyone else. He was followed by Miss Marie Le Blanc—a
lively comedienne. Then came Mr. Harry Freeman—a first-
rate singer of comic songs, to whom I have referred at some
length in an earlier chapter. After Harry, there was Miss
Lily Shaw, programmed as a burlesque artist. Then came the
very quaint, Mr. Fred Earle, whose popular and funny song,
"Seaweed," is still heard in odd places today.

Fred Earle was followed by the dainty and delightful Miss
Ida Rene, who subsequently married the great ventriloquist,
Arthur Prince, and, strangely enough, she was followed in
this particular bill by Lieutenant Cole, a ventriloquist. A
ballad vocalist, Miss Lucy Clarke, was next, and then came
Mr. Harry Tate, not in his famous "Motoring" or "Fishing"
sketches, for which he is best remembered, but billed here
as "The New Mimic," and, believe me, as I have already
told you, Harry was an uncommon specialist in this particular
field.

The Sisters Webster followed Harry, and, by the way,
sister acts were tremendously popular in those days. Afterwards came Mr. Lester King, a baritone, and then, we had a
"Farcical Absurdity" entitled "Touched," performed by
Messrs Keegan, Elvin, and Company. The Elvin referred to
was, of course, the much-loved Joe of that ilk.

Next came the star section of the bill, although I should
point out that many of the artists I have already mentioned
later became major stars in their own right. There was no

intermission in this programme. That great favourite, Miss
Bessie Wentworth, started the star ball rolling, and she was
followed by none other than Mr. Dan Leno—who is simply
programmed as "The Comedian." Then came another sister
act—the Sisters Wynne, described as "The Gaiety Girls,"
and they were followed by that superb descriptive vocalist
Mr. Leo Dryden, always remembered for his "Miner's Dream
of Home."

Afterwards Mr. Gus Elen chased away the tears and pathos,
that Dryden always raised, with his wonderful comedy songs
and character studies: "It's A Great Big Shame," and "If
It Wasn't For the 'Ouses In-Between," to name but two of
these. And then we had the one and only Miss Marie Lloyd—
and I think I have said enough about Marie earlier in this book
not to have to add anything to that. Marie was followed by
Mr. G. W. Hunter—a very clever patter comedian. Then
came The Figaros—"Eccentric Duettists"—and, finally, Mr.
Arthur Rigby, styled as a comic vocalist. It is a coincidence
that, like the first turn on the programme, Horace Mills,
Arthur Rigby later became another of our most notable pantomime dames, and when I watch the famous television serial
of today, "Dixon of Dock Green," and see "Sergeant Flint,"
who is "young Arthur" as I knew him, there are so many
times when he reminds me of his splendid father.

Incidentally, you could see this programme at prices ranging
from sixpence to three shillings, and it was a wonderful
evening's entertainment.

The prefixes "Mister" and "Miss," by the way, were in
general use in the West End music-halls, used, I think, because
they gave dignity to a branch of the profession that was more
often than not looked down upon, especially by the legitimate
theatre heads. The custom died out later, but was always
retained at the London Coliseum and the Palladium. You
might be "Jimmy Riddle" at the Queens in Poplar, but you
were "Mister Jimmy Riddle"—or possibly even "Mister
James Riddle"—at the London Coliseum. Similarly "Hetty

Hangover" at the Putney Hippodrome, would be "Miss Hetty Hangover" at the Palladium!

Another programme which, as a youngster, I saw in company with an indulgent aunt, was at the Palace. This aunt of mine knew the box-office keeper, whose name was Alfred Butt—afterwards, of course, Sir Alfred Butt—who subsequently became the owner of the Palace. A feature of the Palace Theatre programmes at that time, was that they gave the actual times of appearance of each artist, and contemporaries of the period, such as my old friend the late Fred Russell, have told me that they were fairly rigidly adhered to and that there were music-hall goers in those days who would go to a show, simply to see one, or perhaps two, artists, which meant that they could choose the time that their favourites were on. This particular programme was a matinée, and started with the overture prompt at two o'clock and it played for seven minutes. Promptly at two-seven, on came R. H. Douglass, whom I remember as one of the first comedians giving impressions. I won't go through all the names on the bill, but just say that it included that first-class character comedian, George Bastow, of "The Galloping Major," and "Captain Gingah" fame. Then there was Paul Mill, a light comedian, who didn't find the halls much to his liking, but who later became—with Wallis Arthur—one of the pioneers of first-class seaside pierrot parties. Then there was that brilliant mimic, Marie Dainton, who announced that her impressions were given "by kind permission of A. W. Pinero, Esq.; John Hare, Esq.; and George Edwardes, Esq."

At two minutes past four, Mrs. H. Beerbohm Tree was announced, to recite Rudyard Kipling's latest poem—"The Absent-Minded Beggar" (by kind permission of the *Daily Mail*); and then the aforementioned Fred Russell made his appearance at four thirty-three, billed as a ventriloquial comedian. Later, Fred was to be the guide, counsellor, and dearly loved "Uncle Fred" of the Variety Artistes' Federation, and of the Grand Order of Water Rats.

At four forty-five, a great novelty was announced—"The American Biograph"—invented by Herman Casler, of New York, and the list of pictures to be shown included, "Polo at Hurlingham," "A scene from King John" (then playing at Her Majesty's Theatre), "The Daily Mail War Express leaving Great Central Station, London," "Queen Victoria Reviewing the Household Cavalry," "The Landing of General Sir Redvers Bullers at Capetown," "Afternoon Tea in the Gardens of Clarence House," and "Train taking up water at full speed on the London and North Eastern Railway." The prices for this wonderfully varied entertainment, which included eighteen items, ranged from sixpence in the gallery, to seven and sixpence in the fauteuils—or you could get a box for a guinea.

It will give you some idea of the cost of things in those days when I tell you that after the matinée my aunt said: "Now, I promised if you had been good, you could have a special treat for tea before I took you home." "Oh! I have been good, haven't I?" I exclaimed; and my aunt, who liked to put on a severe exterior, but who really had a gentle sense of humour, said: "Yes, you have been fairly good, but very fidgety. However, I am going to take you to Gatti's,"—and off we trudged down the Charing Cross Road, round into the back entrance of Gatti's—the Adelaide Galleries—off the Strand. There my treat was *two* poached eggs on toast—not one, which was my usual allowance at home, on the rather rare occasions I had an egg—and this was followed by luscious cream cakes. When tea was over, I asked for a glass of lemonade. "Tch, tch," said my aunt, "a glass of lemonade after all that tea?" "Well, I feel thirsty," I said. So, after more "tch tchs," the lemonade was brought. My aunt didn't have eggs; in fact, she only had a tea cake, or something like it. When the bill was brought she produced a four-shilling piece, and received some change—and I remember her fiddling about in her purse, trying to find a threepenny bit, but she couldn't, and reluctantly gave a sixpenny tip!

I am browsing over this particular programme in my

20.—MILLICENT MARTIN: the glamorous star from *That Was The Week That Was*

21.—FRANKIE HOWERD: one of our Foremost Funny Men.

bedroom in an hotel—a good hotel, but not the best in this town; the price for this bedroom, with breakfast, is £2 15s. 0d., and it certainly gives one food for thought to see yet another advertisement in this programme, announcing the fact that the Piemont Hotel in Soho Square would provide a bedroom and breakfast for three shillings and sixpence! I am almost nervous of writing down the words "food for thought" in case the particular establishment I am in now charges me for the food! I know this latter price was over sixty years ago; but one wonders if the sheets and blankets, the carpets and curtains, the egg and two pieces of bacon, and the toast—possibly brown on one side and white on the other—have really increased so much in price? True, I have got a basin with running hot and cold water in this room, whereas at the Piemont I expect I should have had a jug and basin, and a Victorian chambermaid would have brought a large brass can of hot water when she called me, but even running hot and cold water is a doubtful blessing, because in the big freeze of 1963 the cold water in the tap was frozen and the boiler which supplied the hot water had burst! Whereas I am sure, in the middle of such a freeze in those earlier days, the hard-worked Victorian servants would, in those deep dungeon-like kitchens, have boiled kettle upon kettle of water for the customers!

CHAPTER XVI

LADIES OF THE PROMENADES

LONG before the music-halls themselves disappeared, the very attractive "ladies" who discreetly dispensed their favours in the promenades and lounges of the "halls"—more especially in London's West End Variety theatres—began to disappear from them, and I should say this exodus was—with isolated exceptions—almost complete by the end of the First World War. At the risk of raising Puritanical and perhaps some hypocritical eyebrows, I must say I have always regretted this, because I felt it robbed these places of a delightfully naughty and exciting atmosphere. The Empire, Leicester Square, and the Alhambra were the principal venues for these meticulously well-behaved "ladies of easy virtue"; here let me pause to say that they were not at all "easy"—and a fellow had to match up to the ladies' assessment both in finance and behaviour before she would condescend to let her virtue be tampered with.

As a young man, when I had some spare cash, I confess I thoroughly enjoyed my visits to the Empire, firstly to watch and revel in Adele Genée's or Yvette Guilbert's magical art and secondly to relax over a glass of draught champagne (where can you find this today?) in that gilt and crystal bar in the company of one of these delightful, glamorous, and often highly intelligent women. Mind you, it didn't always mean that when one of these ladies allowed you, or at times, one might almost say, condescended to let you buy them a drink—that you were fixed up for the night so to speak. Oh dear no! I recall an occasion when a certain scion of a famous family who was standing near me at the bar and was in conversation with one of these ladies, suddenly became rather boisterous, he'd obviously had "one over the eight" and, allowing his amorous feelings to get the better of him, he attempted to kiss her and at the same time put his hand caressingly on her ample behind. And in a flash the lady threw her glass of champagne over him and, calling an attendant, had him removed from the bar. These ladies were a picturesque bevy, beautifully dressed and coiffured and in those large Edwardian hats they really looked most alluring, and most of them would have—and some of them indeed had—graced the best enclosures at Ascot or Goodwood, or were equally at home on lordly yachts at Cowes. Society women of the upper ten—whatever that may have been—might quiz them haughtily through their lorgnettes, but the so called "scarlet" women were quite unperturbed—and went about their unlawful occasions with perfect sang-froid. Why not indeed? They were after all carrying on the traditions of the oldest profession in the world, and doing so with poise and good manners. Moreover they were as discreet as the hall-keeper of any first-class London Club!! A man could take his wife to the Empire or the Alhambra, and if he did by chance run into one of these ladies who might have been the reason for his "being kept late at the office" not a sign of recognition would occur.

Many of them had charming and artistic residences—gener-ally flats—and some of them had maids. There were some who even had a butler! And curiously enough quite a number of these ladies really enjoyed their profession. There was a four-some who had a large mansion in Kensington, in which each one had their separate apartments, their respective ages were roughly between twenty-seven and forty. Each one had their own clientele of patrons. They seldom came to the Empire together, but when they did they came for a "night out" and not to do business, and they were as gay, as happy and as care-free as any bunch of girls who were having an office outing.

They also had a sort of pact and rule, which they rigidly adhered to, this being that once a month they took the week-end off, and as one of them told me, 'From Friday night until Monday lunch time we are 'not at home'."

I learnt that they sometimes went off together for the week-end to Brighton or Margate—and sometimes stayed in town and went to Concerts at the Queen's Hall or the Albert Hall! "Don't you get bored?" I asked Eileen once. "Bored?" she replied. "Good gracious no! We just relax—read—attend to our wardrobe and so on—and it's a delicious experience to go to bed with a book instead of a man."

One of my early experiences with a lady from the Empire taught me a lot. It was about nineteen hundred and eleven, and I was on a visit to London to try and find some work. A benevolent uncle with whom I was staying had augmented my meagre purse and given me four sovereigns. "That's got to last you, my lad," he said, "it'll pay your tram and bus fares and your meals. But if at the end of the week you haven't got an engagement from one of these stupid agents you talk about, then I shall send you back to Liverpool." I well remember that day, tramping round the agents' offices, climbing the stairs, waiting and chafing, hoping that Mr. Blackmore or Mr. St. John Denton or Mr. Weathersby would offer me a job. Alas I had no luck—"Sorry, Mr. Rose," said the urbane Mr. Lionel Wallace of the Blackmore agency—I've filed your particulars—and we'll drop you a line." "Call again next week," said the very busy Mr. Peel, who with an old-world courtesy would grasp you by the hand and make you feel you were the one actor in London that he really wanted to see—and as he gripped you he slowly edged you to the door all the time telling you how glad he was to see you and how well you looked and how excellent the prospects were for you—tomorrow—and by that time he had nearly pushed you down the stairs. It was about five o'clock and I was fed up and decided that whatever the consequences I would have a night out.

But I had my uncle and aunt to consider. Quickly I decided

on my tactics. I took a bus to my uncle's office near London Bridge, and told him a whopping lie. "I think I've fixed an engagement," I said, "but unfortunately Mr. Blackmore's manager wants to take me to see the play he wants me for, and it doesn't start until eight-thirty and won't finish until after eleven; then he has asked me to discuss it with him back at his flat in Maida Vale." I'm afraid I was rather blurred and breathless, but my uncle didn't comment except to say, "Well, you know we go to bed about half-past ten so you'd better stay." And then with what I thought was an amused smile, he took another couple of sovereigns from his purse and said, "Here you are, my boy, you may need these, you never know, and you must always pay your corner." Hurrah! I thought to myself, I'm going to have a real night out. So after a clean-up and spruce at Cannon Street Hotel I made my way to Scott's and had a meal. Hot lobster, a Crème Caramel, Camembert, and half a bottle of Chablis—which cost in those days roughly eleven or twelve shillings!

Then to the Empire! There were some acrobats on when I arrived, but I didn't pay much attention to the show. My mind was on other things, and before the interval I got up and went to the bar. And there *she* was! I'll call her Audrey, though that wasn't her name. Tall, elegant, glorious chestnut hair coiled in a bewitching chignon in her perfectly shaped neck, large violet eyes, full red lips, a typical Edwardian figure, smallish waist and her hips and bosom not too, but sufficiently, ample. For a while I just stood and looked at her and bought myself a glass of champagne. At first she gave me no encouragement, but then came the interval of the show and a rush to the bar, and this was my excuse for moving nearer to her. "Please don't think me very rude," I said nervously, "but I would like to talk to you." "Silly boy," she replied, "I knew you did, but let's go into the promenade, it's a bit crowded here." So to the promenade we went and strolled about until the interval was over and the bar began to empty, whereupon we went back, and Audrey and I had draught champagnes for a while. I was very raw at this sort of thing. Not that I was innocent, but I was uncertain how to make the proper approach to such a lovely and obviously experienced woman. "Where do you live?" I asked. "Why not come home with me and find out?" she replied mischievously, and so after a few preliminaries and inquiries on her part, out we went and she hailed a hansom waiting in the Square. The cabby obviously knew her, because I particularly noticed he didn't inquire for any address. I learnt later that this was quite usual, and that many of these ladies had an arrangement with certain cabbies. She lived in a large flat in Bayswater, at that time known as a very salubrious district. "Give the cabby five shillings," she told me, and I of course obeyed. Quickly she let us in through a big front door, and then led me to her flat on the first floor. It was large, spacious, and furnished in exquisite taste. There was a sort of lounge-dining room which led through double doors to her bedroom, and through the hall there was a splendid bathroom with a hand-worked shower, and next to this another room which I presumed was the maid's.

"There now, Mr. Nervous," she said, "sit down and make yourself at home." She then picked up a little hand-bell which was answered by a trim-looking maid. "Colette," said Audrey, "we'll have supper as soon as possible, and please put out the sherry and glasses now. And for supper we'll have a bottle of the Château Margaux—I shan't be very long," said Audrey, as she handed me a silver box of fat-looking Turkish cigarettes, and disappeared through the double doors to her room. The maid brought in the sherry and poured me out a glass. I lit a cigarette and waited and tried to pretend I was at my ease. Presently Audrey returned. She had changed into a seductive looking *négligée*, and now she kept up a running fire of chatter while she helped the maid to lay the table. The cutlery, the glass and the napery were impeccable, as was the meal—smoked salmon, cold chicken and ham, fresh pineapple and cream, Blue Vinny cheese, and coffee, all washed down with the excellent claret—a "present," she told me, from a well-known wine merchant in the City. She was so attractive, so entertaining and so cultured that I almost forgot the object of my visit in the enjoyment of her animated chatter. How could a delightful creature like this sell herself to different men, I thought, and then I did what many men, especially romantic ones—must have done in similar circumstances. I asked why she did "this sort of thing". She laughed and said, "I knew you'd ask me something of the sort, just as some others have done. I suppose you think I'm far too nice for what you call 'this sort of thing'." "Yes I do," I replied. "Silly boy," she said, "but as you are rather sweetly serious, I'll tell you. I do it because I *like* it— and because by doing it I can enjoy a standard of living and a certain amount of luxury which I want. I was one of George Edward's chorus at the Gaiety," she went on, "and like many of those beautiful girls I got taken out almost nightly after the show—I soon realized that I had no future on the stage—and unlike some of my friends I didn't find a nobleman willing to marry me, although I found several ready to sleep with me. So I made up my mind that if I couldn't have my cake and eat it, I would at any rate have the cake." "Good gracious," I said, "I'm amazed because I'm sure you'd be a wonderful wife." "No you're quite wrong," she said, "I tried it once, but a humdrum though devoted husband and a small semi-detached villa in Lewisham, cured me. I couldn't stand it and I cleared out." "Is your husband still alive?" I asked. "Yes," she said, "he divorced me—but he always sends me a card on my birthday every year." "Well I'm blowed," I could only say. "Yes, I know," she laughed, "and I suppose by now all your passionate ardour has cooled down." She was right and it was more than a couple of hours and several drinks later before I followed her into the bedroom.

During the next two or three years, I saw her on odd visits to London, and always found her the same cheerful and self-contained person and, quite apart from sex, extremely companionable. My excuse for introducing you to her is of course the fact that she and her kind were part and parcel of the West

End music-hall scene, and no narrative about the "halls" would be complete without touching on this subject.

They have gone—as have so many other aspects of London's Bohemian Night Life. The Wolfenden Report has cleared the streetwalkers from the highways, and sent them scurrying underground; and nowadays if you want them, you get their addresses from some scruffy little shop in Soho or some other back street—the type that sell pornographic literature and lewd postcards. The tired business man these days need not be afraid (if indeed he ever was) that he will be accosted in Piccadilly by a lady saying: "Hullo dear, looking for a nice girl?" Instead he can find his excitement in visiting the Strip Tease Clubs or the Keyhole Clubs; or perhaps a sinister looking man, lurking and touting furtively in a dark doorway, will try and induce him to follow him and be assured of some "real fun and games"!

Perhaps we are better off with these new regulations. I don't know, but to my mind Piccadilly and Leicester Square have lost something of their picturesque character. Those saucy naughty "birds" have gone, and the only "birds" you can see there now are those tired-looking blown-up chickens turning over and over while they are roasted in the windows.

And the Empire and the Alhambra are now cinemas—the promenades are gone and with them the elegant courtesans that walked them. And in any case films, coffee and ice-cream are not quite the ideal accompaniment for *les affaires méchantes*.

CHAPTER XVII

STRIKE!

"IT's the first time I have ever heard of actors and variety artists coming out on strike," a well-known south coast resident said to me some time ago. He was referring to the British Actors' Equity stand and fight for better terms, against the Independent Television Authority, which resulted in dozens of artists—great and small—coming out on strike. And they stayed out, until Equity, under the astute, calm, and clear-headed guidance of Mr. Gerald Croasdell, had won certain points.

I informed my friend, of course, that although it was the first time for many years that such a thing had happened, it was not indeed the first time variety artists had come out on strike.

The first music-hall strike commenced on 20 January 1907, and lasted for a period of five weeks—until 25 February. It was a very serious strike, and affected a body of people entirely unfamiliar with anything like trade union customs; there were strong and valid reasons for the strike. Some of the conditions of contracts, and many of the conditions backstage in the music-halls, were, to say the least of it, dreadful, and it must be admitted that many managements—although not all— were slave-drivers in the extreme.

The strike didn't result in the general closure of music-halls, by any means, but it did result in dozens of artists of all types banding together and "coming out"; thus bills at the music-halls were denuded of many famous people. But at first managements didn't budge, because quite a number of artists from the clubs and the concert world, and from other spheres, stepped into the breach, and they were, of course, immediately dubbed blacklegs by the strikers!

Prior to the strike, there was a meeting, on 19 January 1907 at the Surrey Theatre, between the year-old Variety Artistes' Federation, the Amalgamated Musicians' Union, and the National Association of Theatrical Employees, and this meeting required Mr. Walter Gibbons—who, at that time, controlled the interests of the Holborn Empire, the Grand Theatre in Clapham, the Duchess Theatre in Balham, the Ealing Hippodrome, the Empire in Croydon, and the Islington Empire—to sign their charter. If Mr. Gibbons refused to do this, they told him that there would be a strike. The powerful Mr. Gibbons, as I think was expected, was implacable, and refused to sign the charter, and the strike duly commenced on the following day, Monday 20 January.

When one thinks of the conditions demanded by other professions and trades today, the demands of the charter seem quite mild, and very fair. It laid down, *inter alia*, minimum terms and conditions of employment for music-hall artists, musicians and stage-hands, and, above all, it demanded a closed shop. At this time the number of members of the Variety Artistes' Federation had swelled to four thousand odd, and consisted not only of some of the best artists but also some of the best brains in the variety profession.

It was expected that the V.A.F. would regard artists who stepped into the breach during the strike and, in other words, kept the theatres open, as blacklegs, and, although these people didn't regard themselves as such, it would seem that, morally, they were. An interesting sidelight on this strike is that whilst the stoppage was confined to London, it had the full support of the whole country and, in particular, of the then equivalent of the T.U.C., also of many Members of Parliament and several Trades Councils up and down the country. The strikers received cordial messages of support from many industrial unions—including the German Union, which, incidentally, the V.A.F. helped to originate, and also the French Union—and financial support came from many quarters.

The strike, like all strikes, resulted in many hardships and, ironically enough, in many advantages to certain performers who hitherto had been quite unknown, or, at least, unknown as far as the music-halls were concerned, and I will touch on this subject later.

A reference to "blacklegs" is found in a letter to *The Stage*, published in their issue of 7 February 1907; this was from an actor who used the pseudonym of "Unity is Strength," and he deplored the fact that whilst the music-hall artists were making this magnificent stand, a number of actors—twenty at least but probably more—and many of whom he knew personally, had stepped in and taken the place of the strikers at several halls. Just fancy! Mummers from the legitimate theatre, who at that time always looked down upon common music-hall performers and regarded themselves as finer clay, had forgotten all about this professional class distinction, and had seized the opportunity to secure better "lolly" than many of them ever received in their own "Temples of Thespis"—which only goes to show what a strange and changeable bunch of folk we people who strut and fret upon the boards are!

On the same date, *The Stage* also reported that Little Tich, Marie Lloyd, and R. A. Roberts had taken part in a meeting at the Trocadero, seeking to settle the strike with the managements; this was firmly denounced as a lie by all three—and I would love to have heard Marie's denial, in her own vernacular! They promptly put an announcement out to this effect, through the National Alliance, and the same issue reports that the Alliance had expelled Bert Clark from the Federation, for what it termed as "his recent course of action, calculated to be detrimental to the cause."

The chief result of this strike was that it virtually led to the famous Arbitrators Award Contract, for which we have to thank the pioneers of the V.A.F., many of whom worked ceaselessly and selflessly for the benefit of their fellows, led by that great administrator, W. H. Clemart. I have been a member of the Federation for over forty years and was, at one time, on its committee, and I have seen its ups and its downs, its weaknesses and its strength, and I have no time for the odd artist or two who says things like "No—I was a member, but I'm not now; after all, what has the V.A.F. done for me?"— which just goes to show how stupid people can be, and makes one wonder what they expect.

But the plain fact is that the conditions established by the Arbitrators Award, and engineered by the V.A.F., were a benefit to all of us, and although, unfortunately, there are few music-halls left today, the Federation is still alive and kicking; and, under the able guidance of its General Secretary, R. W. Swinson, M.B.E., the presidency of Dave O'Gorman—son of Joe O'Gorman, who was one of the fighters for the cause— and the chairmanship of Jimmy Edwards—who, by the time this is published, might well have to add the letters M.P. after his name—is doing a grand job.

But to get back to the "blacklegs"; there were several of these, but one in particular was a great friend and brother Savage of mine, the late Tom Clare, a first-class entertainer at the piano, who came from a Broadstairs concert party— which, by the way, was a miniature nursery for artists who made a name for themselves, such as W. H. Berry and James Blakeley. Tom had been a popular entertainer at London dinners and concerts, and seized the opportunity the strike gave him. He always defended his action to me on the grounds that he was not a member of the V.A.F., and that anyone was entitled to offer him a job, and he was entitled to accept it. Anyway it wasn't long before he was a top-of-the-bill feature all over London and the provinces. And he came into the halls at a time when there were some first-class entertainers at the piano, such as Barclay Gammon, Cooper Mitchell, Nelson

Jackson, Leslie Harris, Margaret Cooper, Harry Fragson, and many others. They, of course, were following in the heritage left by such famous entertainers at the piano as Corney Grain, George Grossmith, Senior, and Mel B. Spurr. Although these latter were not essentially music-hall entertainers they were in the top class of what were then called "Society Entertainers." In passing, one wonders whether the quiet style and intelligent song lyrics of those days would appeal to a generation of which a large section are bred on pops and juke boxes.

In these days, when strikes are almost as frequent an epidemic as the common cold, this particular music-hall strike may sound strangely bizarre and unreal, and unimportant— a bunch of happy-go-lucky Bohemian men and women of varying nationalities, banding together and making a stand for their rights; and, believe me, we are a difficult breed to get together on anything definite! It seems—as it seemed then to some people—almost impossible, but though it was nearly sixty years ago, and in the days when the theatre and the music-hall were regarded as a profession, and not—as today— as "show business," those of us who can still find work in any music-hall that is left, or in the newer media of television, radio, or films, are still enjoying many of the benefits secured for us by those pioneer founders—and we do, indeed, owe them a debt of very great gratitude.

CHAPTER XVIII

AN OLD DATE BOOK

An old date book I came across the other day among my
relics is probably more indicative of the changing face of
entertainment today than any other factor, and, browsing
through it, I feel it reads like an obituary to the death of
variety and the disappearance of music-halls.

The year is 1919 and it shows that the double act of Fox and
Rose had bookings to play for three years ahead at the follow-
ing halls in London alone: the Chiswick Empire, Shepherd's
Bush Empire, Hammersmith Palace, Putney Hippodrome,
Penge Empire, Hackney Empire, Kilburn Empire, Walham
Green Empire, Willesden Hippodrome, Lewisham Hippo-
drome, Camberwell Palace, New Cross Empire, Stratford
Empire, Chelsea Palace, Brixton Empress, Tottenham Palace,
East Ham Palace, Walthamstow Palace, the Granville (Wal-
ham Green), Finsbury Park Empire, South London Palace,
Kingston Empire, Rotherhithe Hippodrome, Woolwich
Empire, Olympia (Shoreditch), Empire (Croydon), Grand
(Clapham), the Euston, Islington Empire, and the Metro-
politan (Edgware Road)! Just imagine—thirty weeks in one's
own home and one's own bed, and a full book of work!
This list does not, of course, exhaust all the suburban music-
halls, and does not include the West End ones, like the
Holborn, the Palladium, the Coliseum, the Alhambra, and the
Victoria Palace.

And then there were the provincial halls, controlled by

Moss Empires, the Stoll Circuit, and the MacNaghton Circuit, and the large number of independent ones. Today there is not a single music-hall left in London, because the Palladium —although it does present variety—is no longer a music-hall in the fullest sense of the word; it is a number-one production house. Makes you think, doesn't it?

And this brings me to the recent closing of the Metropolitan—known the world over as "The Met." This took place on Good Friday, 12 April 1963, and it is fitting that its last performance should have been an all-star show in aid of the music-hall's own charity—the old people's home at Twickenham, known throughout the profession as "Brinsworth"—a real haven for aged variety artists who, through the ups-and-downs of our strange profession, need the help and care that the Variety Artistes' Benevolent Fund can give them —not only through the home itself, but with grants to all deserving cases.

It was a night of sadness and joy—a night of memories, sweet sentiment, and fond regret. The theatre was packed, and hundreds of people had to be turned away. How strange it is, and how ironical, that people will always turn up for an occasion such as a funeral or a memorial service; and one reflects that if only they had supported the Met with the same enthusiasm during its last declining years, we should not have been watching its final variety programme. As Mr. Victor Wilson, the general manager, said: "Everyone wants to come on a night like this; if they had been in here years ago, we wouldn't be closing tonight."

There was laughter, there was applause, and there were tears in this theatre where the great names of variety had strutted its boards. And perhaps it was fitting that the programme included not only stars of former generations but also of the present. No one better than the brilliant Tommy Trinder could have been found to take charge and compère, and with his own inimitable manner he combined brilliantly the obvious nostalgia of the occasion with his own infectious humour. Hetty King, Issy Bonn, and Ida Barr brought the tang of former days, and in contrast Johnny Lockwood, Wyn Calvin, Mrs. Shufflewick, Dickie Valentine, Eddie Reindeer, Ted Ray, and many others gave us the punch of the present, making a perfect blend for an unforgettable occasion; and under the expert musical direction of Ivan Dozin the whole show went without a hitch.

When I first played the Met that great character the lovable Bill Bailey was the manager, shortly to be assisted by the dapper Billy Matthew. Bill Bailey always wore a frock-coat that was turning slightly green and a top-hat that sometimes looked as if it had been brushed the wrong way—a great contrast to the immaculate Billy Matthew, resplendent in the latest-cut tails, sparkling linen, and shining top-hat that you could see your face in! Bill Bailey was a true music-hall manager, and on our first visit gave the Fox and Rose act some good tips. The star attraction that particular week was that great handler of songs, Victoria Monks, known as "John Bull's Girl," and there was indeed, a bull-doggish attack in all Vicky Monks's work. "Won't You Come Home, Bill Bailey?" she sang, and its recent revival with current pop singers—famous and otherwise—still leaves her rendition unequalled.

It was the custom in those days for the artists to pop on an overcoat and a muffler or a wrap and go through, in their make-up, to that big circular bar, and many were the amusing—and sometimes very voluble—moments when Vicky Monks gave us her colourful points of view! This bar was possibly the favourite haunt, not only of the public, but of the profession; managers, agents, Press, artists—all would congregate there, night after night; you could always bet on seeing some crony or other.

I thought of this, and many other similar happy times, as I stood outside, and looked at the posters for the final show; and I knew for certain that all those who through the years had played the Met were glad that the proceeds of this show—which I will call a "Requiem for the Met"—were for the

Variety Artistes' Benevolent Fund, and its home for pros—
Brinsworth.

Brinsworth started in quite a small way in 1910, and here
we must raise our hats to Harry Marlow, its indefatigable
secretary for many years. Harry Marlow was what was known
as a "light comedian" in those days, and when he had some
good songs he was quite a pleasant entertainer—never hitting
the high-spots, but generally making a useful contribution to
a variety programme. But it was as the General Secretary of
the Variety Artistes' Benevolent Fund that he will be chiefly
remembered. He was a great organizer, and an enthusiastic
worker, and in the arranging of notable Royal Performances
and other functions he certainly put Brinsworth on the map.
It is therefore with no disregard or disrespect to his efforts and
memory that I say that, although Brinsworth served a grand
purpose as an institution, it was not until Arthur Scott became
its secretary, that it really became a home, in the fullest meaning of the word, and I attribute this fact to the way that
Arthur and his wife Betty immediately brought a "Mum and
Dad" atmosphere to the place, and by the warmth of their
own personalities, their long experience of brother and sister
pros, and their poised and gracious outlook on life they have
made those who live under the Brinsworth roof almost feel
like honoured guests!

Brinsworth itself has quite recently been altered, modernized and transformed architecturally and in furnishing, and
this, of course, is splendid; but the most important trans-
formation, in my opinion, is this "Mine Host and Hostess"
influence that Arthur and Betty have infused. It was my
privilege, when I was presenting *Twinkle* at Worthing on
several occasions, to invite my fellow pros from Brinsworth
to have a day out, so to speak, and come down and see the
show, and it was a joy to see the unobtrusive care and attention
bestowed on them by Arthur and Betty, and the affection and
respect that these good people had for them was very evident.

The last time they came, I took that one-time splendid

9

comic, Jack Edge, out for a drink. "Are you happy at Brinsworth, Jack?" I asked. "Clarkie," he replied, "I never knew
what real happiness and peace were until I came to Brinsworth."
And this was from a man who for many years was one of our
leading pantomime and variety artists, a chap who had lived
in the best hotels, and who had tasted all the luxuries of life;
and it speaks not only for itself, but is an eloquent tribute to
Brinsworth's "Mum and Dad"—Arthur and Betty Scott.

Yes, the strongholds of the music-hall disappear, the bastions fall, and this was further emphasized shortly after the
Met's last show, when, once again, Tommy Trinder went to
Collins' Music-Hall in Islington, to auction photographs,
playbills, and other relics, that had for years adorned the bars
and vestibules of this historic house. The proceeds of this
auction, too, were for the V.A.B.F. "We expected to get about
a hundred pounds," said Arthur Scott—but he had reckoned
without the Trinder touch! Taking over from the official
auctioneer early in the proceedings, Tommy cajoled seven
hundred and fifty pounds from the customers! Holding up
a photograph of Dr. Crippen's wife, Belle Elmore, he said:
"Here's a photograph of Belle Elmore—autographed at a
Water Rats Ball, the night before Crippen 'did' her!" This
fetched thirty-five pounds, which only goes to show how
being "done" can enhance the value of a photo! Far more
relative to real value, was the drawing of Past King Rat,
Harry Tate; this fetched sixty pounds, and no one was more
pleased about this than his son Ronnie, when he heard the
news.

Tommy poked audacious fun when he held up a picture of
Jimmy Jewell, Ben Warriss, and Jimmy Wheeler. Adopting
the manner of the market-place "quack doctor," he said:
"I have 'ere, ladies and gentlemen, a valuable antique; it is a
picture of three illustrious stars, all in one frame—Jimmy
Jewell, Ben Warriss, and Jimmy Wheeler." There was silence;
no bid came from the audience. "Blimey! No bid for this
unique and unforgettable picture—a picture you will never

have the chance of seeing again, and I will tell you for why: Jimmy Jewell is wearing a National Health wig, and won't be photographed any more; Jimmy Wheeler may not be able to stand up to be photographed, and Ben Warriss is so bloody ugly, that no photographer will risk his camera on him these days!" And with similar leg-pulling and fun throughout the day Tommy added another Trinder triumph to his already long list, and a very unexpected windfall for Brinsworth!

CHAPTER XIX

THAT WAS VARIETY—THAT WAS!

AND so we near the end of our journey down Memory Lane, and I hope you will agree that we have met many rich and unique characters on our way. My only regret is that there are so many more that I would like you to have met, and, every now and then, as I have been writing this narrative, I got a jolt or two that reminded me of more delightful people, places, and customs, and I said to myself: "Fancy having overlooked him or her or that!"

As, for instance, my experience with Horatio Bottomley, an M.P. at one time, who was one of the most powerful voices through the medium of his *John Bull* magazine and his platform speeches in the country. He engaged me for one or two private functions, always treated me kindly, and always paid me more than my fee and made me share his champagne! In spite of his faults and subsequent downfall, it should not be forgotten that at the start of the First World War his recruiting speeches brought thousands to the colours. He was a rogue, if you like—full of bluff—but, as Queenie Leighton used to sing: "There's a Little Bit of Good in the Worst of Us"— and there was a lot of good in Horatio Bottomley. So big was his name that, in a revue of the time at the Vaudeville Theatre, that clever light comedian, Clay Smith, sang a song called "If It's In *John Bull* It *Is* So"—which was the slogan of Bottomley's newspaper. I added several verses to it, and Bottomley always made me sing it when he engaged me, and when

I went to visit him at Parkhurst he rather pathetically asked me to sing some of it again—which I did.

And I haven't told you about Bernard Shaw, who took a kindly, though intermittent, interest in me from the time when I played the Jewish Doctor in *The Doctor's Dilemma* at Liverpool. Years later, on Eastbourne Pier, he was able, with his amazing memory, to tell me all about it!

When I was running my own pantomimes at the King's Theatre in Hammersmith I wrote to him: "You have written most things in your life, sir—why don't you write me a pantomime?" And one of his famous postcard replies now adorns my study wall. Dated 5 September 1947, it reads: "Nonsense, Rose!—a man does not start writing pantomimes at ninety-one! G.B.S."

Neither have you met John Bodkin Adams, who has been my doctor for thirty years. If there was such a position or post as an "Actor's Doctor and Physician," I would like to see John Bodkin, as I always call him, in the job. A big and burly Belfast Irishman, somewhat detached and shy, he, to my mind, is uncanny in the way he diagnoses immediately physical and mental illness. The public image evoked of him by his trial for murder was entirely false, and also there is no doubt in my mind that his dedication to his work caused antagonism in circles that should have known better. I never knew a man put in such long hours at his practice and at hospitals, through the days—and nights, when necessary; there isn't a time on the clock when you can't call him and find him immediately ready to bring you succour and comfort. And, strangely enough, although medicine is his business, he won't give you any unless it is absolutely necessary. He has often given me a cure with his homely and commonsense chats. I kept in touch with him the whole time during the trial, and when he was in Brixton Jail, and I treasure the letters he wrote me from there—a true revelation of a faith and a character that kept him going and saw him through the valley.

I would like you to have met Dean Inge, known as the "Gloomy Dean." Gloomy or not, he enjoyed comic songs, and, knowing this, I one day said to him: "You must give me a photograph, and I shall hang it in my study, between those of George Robey and Harry Randall." He was quite non-plussed, and obviously unaccustomed to such requests, but he gave me a very old faded picture on which he wrote: "An old one, but it's the only one I've got— W. R. Inge."

And I would like you to have come with me to a great American artist's dressing-room, at the London Coliseum, and have listened to the imperious Norah Bayes ordering her dresser—a veritable coal-black mammy—to give me some "korfee," while she listened almost humbly as I cheekily told her to discard the blonde wig she wore in her act and show her own lovely grey hair. "You don't mean that, Clarkson?" she said. "Well, Miss Bayes," I replied, "you honoured me by asking me to watch your act and tell you what I thought because you were disappointed at its reception, and I have just given you my humble opinion." And, may I say, when later she moved over to the Palladium, she did as I suggested, and it really did help this magnificent artist to pack this theatre for months.

I would like you also to have been with me at the Houses of Parliament when Alfred Denville gave me lunch, and introduced me to Jimmy Maxton and Ernest Bevin. There was a purpose behind this invitation of Alfred's. Chatting with Ernest Bevin afterwards I learnt that he wanted me to delete a few lines from my topical "Rule Britannia" song, which poked fun at Mr. Attlee and Mr. Shinwell. Ernest Bevin was a staunch lover and supporter of the music-hall, and he had heard me sing this song at Alfred's Harrow Coliseum theatre. Alfred had previously asked me to delete the lines, and I had said: "No, Alfred. It's only fun, and you wouldn't mind fun being poked at a Tory, and you mustn't mind it being poked at the Labour blokes!" I argued with Ernest Bevin, and he, big-hearted and broad-minded man that he was, saw my point of view. Ernest Bevin was unique in the fact that though his life had been one long battle for his convictions he could always see the other fellow's point of view.

Another great friend of mine, and indeed, a great friend of many of my theatre and music-hall colleagues, was that brilliant solicitor, A. E. Fournier, known to all as "Bert" Fournier. I have never been a good businessman, and Bert crossed my horizon at a time when my affairs were in a sorry state. He, with his knowledge, his care, and his ferret-like ability, extricated me from a lot of trouble. Here again was a shy man. Meeting him casually one would never have thought that he was the guide, counsellor, and friend to innumerable stars and managements. He had a tremendous love of the theatre, plus a vast knowledge, and had he not been a lawyer he could, in my opinion, have been a wonderful impresario because he had an uncanny instinct of knowing what was good and what was bad in shows. His son, Maurice, obviously caught the theatre bug from his father, and is today a prominent producer; his other son, Bill, I am grateful to say, carries on the great Fournier legal tradition.

No narrative about variety would be complete without a reference to the late Max Miller. I am writing these words shortly after his funeral at Brighton, and I write them not only with the sadness at the passing of a colleague whom I knew very well, but also with the sadness that, with his passing, we have lost one of the few remaining stalwarts of variety. Greater pens than mine, and more important voices, have paid tribute to his artistry.

Max was not a man who mixed very freely in the profession; success and affluence often breeds envy and unjustified unpopularity and criticism from one's fellows, and Max often suffered from such injustice as this. And yet I happen to know his private benefactions and help to those in need were wide and numerous. When it was my job to present star guest-artists on Sundays at Eastbourne Pier, Max Miller was at the height of his fame, but the Pier directors were angry with me for booking him. "He is so vulgar and suggestive," said the managing director. "Don't worry," I replied, "Max will do as I ask him." "Nobody will come and see him," was the retort. In point of fact he packed the Pavilion, and broke all records. I had explained to him that I could not possibly afford his normal fee, but that he would enhance my prestige very much if he would come. And I know he wouldn't have minded my telling you that he came to me for what amounted to an expense fee of thirty pounds, at a time when his fee for such an appearance was never less than a hundred guineas! And, what is more, he so enjoyed himself with the, at first, apprehensive and "look-see" Eastbourne audience, whom he captivated and devastated completely, that, at the end he said: "Clarkie, I want to come again." And come again he did at the same fee, and again he broke all records, including his own!

Living with him at various places on tour we would chat far into the night, and he delighted in getting out his ukelele and trying out ideas on me. I was always convinced that he didn't really understand some of the outrageous things he said he was going to say and sing! No, believe it or not, Max was a mixture of cockney cheekiness and yet complete naïveté, and, in my opinion, it was this mixture that made his act—audacious as it was—completely inoffensive to a healthy and broad-minded audience. There was none of the leer of the old-time comics—no red noses, or battered hat—and the blatant silks and satins of his attire, the immaculate stockings and shoes, the perfectly groomed head, and the smart hat tilted on one side, plus a winning and disarming smile was the cleverly conceived paraphernalia that made "The Cheeky Chappie" supreme in his generation. As my friend Alfred Marks so rightly said in his radio tribute: "Music-halls started to close ten years ago, but they died this afternoon when they buried Max Miller."

But as always, particularly in the entertainment world, it is a case of "the show must go on," and when a gloomy old-stager to whom I was showing the "Oxford" programme, referred to in Chapter XIV, said to me: "You couldn't get a programme as good as that today, whatever you may say, Clarkie," I replied—"Nonsense! Why not!" "What!" he exclaimed, "over twenty-one acts, and all of 'em good, *and* different—where are they?" "Where are they?" I repeated, and, taking a sheet of paper from the Club table, I wrote down the following names: Max Bygraves, Ted Ray, Norman Wisdom, Shirley Bassey, Bruce Forsyth, Jimmy James and Company, Beryl Reid, Ken Dodd, Arthur Haynes and Company, Adele Leigh, Tommy Cooper, Arthur Askey, Margot Henderson, Morecambe and Wise, Dickie Valentine, Edmund Hockridge, Millicent Martin, Frankie Howerd, Dora Bryan, Roy Castle, Dickie Henderson, Shani Wallis, Tommy Steele, Yana, and The Tiller Troupe. "There you are," I said, handing it to him, "and with Tommy Trinder to act as chairman-compère, so to speak, you have got a bunch there that couldn't be bettered in any age—and, what is more, I could more than duplicate them with many other wonderful present-day artists and acts that I have left out, and if that wasn't enough, what about the splendid Black and White Minstrels? There's a show that embodies tip-top variety, combining vocalism, dancing, comedy, and colour in a brilliant fast-moving panorama, and for the lovers of nostalgia the bulk of the songs they use are old faithfuls. No, indeed, it is simply ridiculous to live in the past."

We must stop now, because there is still another chapter to write and the publisher will probably assume that I am doing dear old Herschel Henlere's act—that great entertainer, and still greater character, who climbed from the honky-tonks of America and Canada to international stardom. Audiences can never have enough of him, and Hersch, in a haze of sheer enjoyment, can never have enough of them! Clocks don't matter to him, and he often extensively exceeds his allotted time with an exuberant enthusiasm, and on one occasion an irate management chucked him the key of the theatre, and left him at it! I don't want the publisher to do that to me, so I will bring this chapter to a hasty close!

CHAPTER XX

MEET MR. SHOWBUSINESS!

Mr. Showbusiness . . . in other words—Billy Butlin! In these current years of grace Bill Butlin stands alone in undisputed claim and possession of this title. Not that titles worry Bill—I'm sure they don't—and in any case he could lay claim to so many that I don't suppose the odd one here and there ever bothers him. He has been labelled Mr. Happiness, Mr. Holidays, Mr. Showman, and so on, and the best assessment of this remarkable man can be found in Rex North's delightful book: *The Butlin Story*. But it is about his influence and his tremendous impact on the variety profession that I want to talk, and in these days when the bastions and strongholds of variety are falling fast—when a variety programme in a music-hall is as rare as a Tory vote in Ebbw Vale—it is a comforting and warming thought to know that Bill Butlin—the world's greatest showman—is on our side.

Not so very long ago a variety artist could work in the music-halls controlled by the big combines, such as Moss Empires, The Stoll Theatres, the Syndicate Halls, and various provincial circuits for weeks on end, but nowadays as far as variety is concerned, they are almost a thing of the past. The Palaces, the Hippodromes, and the Empires all over the country have been swallowed up by the development octopus, but thanks to this great showman the Butlin Empire not only survives but extends its borders every year.

In 1962 I was regretting the passing of the Finsbury Park

Empire in a chat with a well-known variety comic. "I should worry," he said jauntily, "I'm booked solid for the next five months." "Where?" I asked, somewhat surprised. "Butlin's in Skegness," he replied. "Got my contract today, and believe me I haven't had five *weeks*, let alone five months, in my date-book for years." That cryptic conversation will give you some idea of what Bill Butlin means to our calling— and he means a lot more than the usual employer of our services.

I have never had the pleasure of working for him, which has been my loss, but so many of my colleagues who have done so have told me in glowing and enthusiastic terms that it is entirely different from working in the usual spheres. "You feel you are part of a large family," said that gay Irish Entertainer the late Jack Daly, "and you feel you want to do more than your usual job to please Daddy—in other words Billy himself." And just before he died Norman Evans, that great comedian and pantomime dame, wrote to me from Butlin's Pwllheli Camp where he was playing for the season. "I have played in the best theatres and music-halls in the world," he wrote, "and you can take it from me, Clarkie, that working in a Butlin theatre is a terrific experience, and although I've not been too well, I've never been happier in my life." One of the most respected men in the variety profession is Harry Morris, of that well-known vintage double-act, Morris and Cowley, an act that has graced music-hall bills for nearly half a century; and Harry, who has the honoured post of Scribe Rat to the Grand Order of Water Rats, is never given to effusiveness or blah-blah. He has this to say about Billy Butlin: "We have appeared at the Butlin Camps for many years—in fact we appeared in his Skegness theatre before it was in the camp and was open to the general public—and believe me the treatment, the efficiency and the on-the-spot care given to all artists, great and small, is truly wonderful, and the know-how of Billy Butlin is evidenced by the splendid body of men he has chosen to administrate his entertainment department. It is the greatest possible joy to work in a Butlin theatre. You don't feel, as many artists must have felt in recent years, that you are just another act from the assembly line of a remote head office. Rather do you feel that Billy himself has chosen you for this or that particular theatre because he likes your act and knows his customers will like it. His personality pervades performers and audiences alike in all his theatres in much the same way, but in a larger sense, that the late Sir Oswald Stoll's personality and ideas pervaded his theatres in other days. The comparison ends there, for while Sir Oswald was undoubtedly a great and revolutionary magnate of the music-hall, and gave to its artists and audiences many benefits, he remained an aloof and austere person, in complete contrast to the warm hearted Billy Butlin.

Derek Salberg—impresario and managing director of Birmingham's famous Alexandra Theatre—said in a recent speech: "Theatres are like human beings—they need love, care, and attention." How right he was; and while many of the big combines have sometimes forgotten this—and it may partly have been one of the reasons why so many of their theatres have closed—Billy Butlin has made love and care a number one priority, with the result that though theatres and music-halls all over the country are closing or being pulled down Bill is building new ones every year: and of course he has this great advantage—he not only supplies the shows but he also supplies the audience.

But great showman that he is, when he talks about his activities and experiences there is a complete absence of the usual showman's boasting. Instead one finds a simple frankness and charm that is most engaging, as for instance when he relates how he sent Frankie Howerd up to Filey soon after the war to give him a trial—and incidentally what a wonderful stepping-stone this was for Frankie "on his way to the forum" in which he emerges as possibly our finest funny man. Then Bill will talk of the time when Charlie Drake, Des O'Connor, Russ Hamilton, and Cliff Richard were Redcoats—or of the difficult period after the war when pros were trying to find their feet. Yes, it was Butlin's Camps that provided the springboard as it were for chaps like Bill Maynard, Dennis Spicer, Terry Scott, Hugh Lloyd, and Norman Vaughan, to name only a few, and as for the "beat brigade"—well, the Springfields (a top vocal group until October 1963), Joe Brown, Brian Poole, and Ringo Starr (now one of the famous Beatles) all had seasonal jobs entertaining in the bars of Bill's camps. In fact it is no exaggeration when I say that Bill Butlin's Camps have for long been the nursery, the graduation school, and the university for such a lot of us. Moreover the talent competitions he runs weekly at all his camps, in conjunction with the *People* newspaper, are a splendid medium for giving new talent a grand opportunity under ideal conditions. From these the winners from each camp go on to the northern and southern semi-finals, and the successful competitors are then through to the grand finals which are held in a West End theatre every year. I frankly admit that until I had begun my research at the Butlin Headquarters—where I received the charming and invaluable help of Lieut.-Col. Basil Brown, Bill's Head of Entertainments—I hadn't realized what the Butlin Camps mean to all branches of our profession.

Come round the coast with me and see the luxurious theatres at Ayr, Mosney, Pwllheli, Minehead, Bognor Regis, Brighton, Clacton, Margate, Filey, and Skegness—all presenting entertainment in all its forms: star guest nights, resident revues, concert parties, children's shows, resident repertory companies, and cabarets. World-famous stars from all spheres of showbusiness have appeared and are appearing at Butlin's. To name all of them here would be like preparing an index for "Who's Who in Showbusiness," but browsing through a recent list of names I see Roy Castle, Rosemary Squires, Jimmy James, Lenny the Lion, Arthur Worsley, Jimmy Wheeler, Stan Stennett, Dennis Spicer, Jon Pertwee, and many others; and these stars are only part of the shows—dozens of small acts are needed to support them, plus a hundred or so glamorous girls for the dancing troupes. Then

there are forty top bands to supply the music, plus M.Cs and
compères, etc., and always the redoubtable Redcoats—Billy
Butlin's pride, and rightly so, because apart from their many
duties as hosts and hostesses of happiness they give first-class
presentations with their own units.

What sort of man is this Billy Butlin? This man who from
small beginnings dreamed his dreams, built his castles (his
camps) in the air, and by his uncanny intuition, instinct, and
industry saw the dreams come true and the castles built. Well,
I say again, read Rex North's *Butlin Story* from which you will
get a vivid picture of the man and the magnate—drawn by a
writer who has been Bill's personal friend for twenty-odd
years. Compared with this my own knowledge of him is
based on three or four meetings and the interest and observation that men like Billy Butlin inspire in those of us who want
to learn. He is a cherished Companion of the Grand Order of
Water Rats and I first met him in one of our Lodge meetings.
I was at once impressed by the unobtrusive manner in which
this important man almost effaced himself. Bill has weight,
both in physical bulk and character, to throw about but he
never does so, and on receiving a specially warm welcome back
to Lodge (an old Water Rats' custom) he made the briefest
and humblest of replies, and sat down.

Some time later when I asked his help and advice in the
preparation of my book *Beside the Seaside* he gave me his blessing
and help. Subsequently I've met him for odd moments at
social functions, and quite recently he gave me an interview.
Here let me digress for a moment and say I've always found
the busiest and most important people, in spite of rigid
business time-tables, are the ones who can always find time to
give a lesser person—which reminds me of what the late
Sir Oswald Stoll once said to me when I thanked him rather
effusively for giving me an interview: "I don't know how to
thank such a busy man as yourself, Sir Oswald, for finding
time to see me." "I should not be able to hold my position
today, Mr. Rose," he replied, "if I had not been able to find

time wherever necessary. Time should be one's slave—not one's master."

But to get back to this last meeting with Bill. My appointment was for eleven o'clock on a Monday morning. Promptly at five to eleven I presented myself at the Butlin Headquarters in Oxford Street. I had never been there before and was at once impressed, not only with the air of busy efficiency, but also by a make-yourself-at-home atmosphere which is immediately conveyed by those charming Redcoat ladies and the rest of the staff, and it seemed fitting that on a raised plinth at the back of the reception counter a big brass bust of Billy Butlin should be presiding over his kingdom as it were. At eleven o'clock I was taken up in a lift to his sanctum. There he was behind his desk in his shirt-sleeves. He had just returned overnight from a hectic social and business week-end in York. "You must be tired out with all that work and rushing about!" I said. "It's not my work that tires me," he laughed, "it's my pleasures."

Briefly I related the object of my visit. He listened carefully and again gave me his O.K. and blessing, and calling in his faithful aide-de-camp, Harold Vinter, he handed me over. "Harold," he said, "give Clarkie all the particulars he wants." And then, as members of his staff came popping in with plans, figures, and what have you for the boss's attention, we said good-bye. "Go and have a coffee and come back in an hour and see Harold," he said, and with a cordial handshake I left him. But I did not go and have a coffee. No, instead I went down to the reception office, sat down, and spent a most entertaining and instructive hour watching the different types of people coming in and out, each one receiving the personal attention of a smiling Redcoat cheerfully answering their inquiries, dealing with their requirements and problems with serene patience—treating all and sundry as if they were the only persons who mattered, and sending them away obviously infected with the spirit of companionship and happiness which seems to be Billy Butlin's own secret formula.

Harold Vinter took a great deal of trouble to supply me with the data I wanted, and I left the Butlin Headquarters grateful for an exhilarating experience in meeting a man of the people, catering for the people, and, to paraphrase Abraham Lincoln's famous words, his aim is to please all of the people all of the time.

You will see now why I titled this chapter "Meet Mr. Showbusiness," because it is Billy Butlin who has been keeping variety's flag flying more than anyone else. He has paid out thousands of pounds in salaries to performers of all types—those on the way up the ladder, those at the top of the ladder, and those on the way down. Yes indeed! And for some of these latter, who for various reasons were not employable in their own line, he has found jobs and niches in his camps.

His generosity and benefactions are widespread and almost without parallel, and he has infused our business with the unbounded buoyancy and opulent optimism of his own dynamic outlook and spirit, and the world in general, and the world of showbusiness in particular is a better world for the presence therein of Billy Butlin.

INDEX

Adams, John Bodkin, 133
Adeler and Sutton, 63
Afton, Richard, 76
Albert and Edmunds troupe, 21
Alexander of Hillsborough, Viscount, 90
Alexandra Theatre, Birmingham, 34, 141
Alhambra Theatre, Leicester Square, 59, 62, 70, 108, 114, 120, 126
Allen, Chesney, 86
Amalgamated Musicians' Union, 122
André, Victor, 101
Andrew, Prince, 100
Anne, H.R.H. Princess, 99
Arbitrators Award Contract, 124
Argyle, the, Birkenhead, 58
Argyll, Duchess of, 98
Armstrong, Barney, 87
Arnold, Tom, 90
Arthur, Wallis, 82, 111
Ashcroft, Dame Peggy, 18
Askey, Arthur, 42-3, 99, 137
Astor, A. C. (Arthur), 93, 101
Austin, Charlie, 92-5

Bailey, Bill, 128
Bard, Wilkie, 13, 24, 57, 96
Barr, Ida, 128
Barrasford tour, 21, 60
Barrett, Wilson, 15
Bassett, Leon, 56
Bassey, Shirley, 19, 137
Bastow, George, 111
Baxter, Stanley, 37
Bayes, Norah, 134
Beatles, the, 142
Beauchamp, George, 21, 22
Bellwood, Bessie, 21
Bennett, Billy, 43-4
Bernhardt, Sarah, 57, 96
Berry, W. H., 124
Besses O' The Barn, 16
Bevin, Ernest, 134-5
"Bing Boys", 62, 70

Birmingham, 22, 23, 76
Birmingham Empire, 33
Black and White Minstrel Show, 37
Black and White Minstrels, 137
Blackmore agency, 116
Blakeley, James, 124
Boissets, the, 21
Bonehill, Bessie, 21
Bonn, Issy, 128
Bottomley, Horatio, 132
Brantford, Tom, 87
Brighton Palace Pier, 79
Brinsworth, 129-31
British Actors' Equity, 121
Brixton Empress, 126
Broadhead Circuit, 21, 61
Brown, Lieut.-Col. Basil, 142
Brown, Joe, 142
Burdon, Albert, 40
Burgess, Lilian, 101
Butlin, W. E. (Billy), 90, 139-45
Butt, Sir Alfred, 58, 111
Byfield, Jack, 86
Bygraves, Max, 18, 38, 78, 86, 99, 137
Byng, George, 56

Calvert, Eddie, 99
Calvin, Wyn, 128
Camberwell Palace, 126
Campbell, Donald, 99
Campbell, Herbert, 73
Canterbury music-hall, 21, 35
Carl Rosa Opera Company, 16
Carpenter, Freddie, 38
Carte, D'Oyly, 16
Casler, Hermann, 112
Castle, Roy, 137, 142
Castling, Harry, 52
Cavanagh, Peter, 99
Chairman, the, 22-3
Chaplin, Charlie, 92-5
Charles, H.R.H. Prince, 99
Chelsea Palace, 126
Chester, Charlie, 86, 98, 99
Chevalier, Albert, 53, 95-6

Chinn, J. Rosser, 91
Chirgwin, the White Eyed Kaffir, 57
Chiswick Empire, 59, 60, 126
Churchill, Sir Winston, 97
Cinquavali, Paul, 21
Clare, Tom, 104, 124
Clark, Bert, 123
Clarke, Denny, 58-9
Clarke, Lucy, 109
Clemart, W. H., 124
Clubs, 20, 23-4
Coburn, Charles, 54
Cochran, C. B., 40
Cogan, Alma, 20, 99
Cole, Lieutenant, 109
Collins, Pat, 16
Collins' Music-Hall, 55, 130
Compton, Fay, 57
Cooper, Margaret, 125
Cooper, Tommy, 14, 99, 137
Covent Garden Opera House, 104
Covery, Thomas, On the Dole, 40
Crazy Gang, 59, 103
Crippen, Dr., 29, 130
Croasdell, Gerald, 121
Crocker, Mr., 102
Cruikshank, Stewart, 37, 38
Curtis-Bennett, Sir Noel, 89

Dagmar, Alexandra, 21
Daily Mail, the, 17, 111
Dainton, Marie, 111
Dale and O'Malley, 22
Daly, Dutch, 57
Daly, Jack, 140
Damerell, Stanley, 93
Datas, the memory man, 57
David, Worton, 52
Delfont, Bernard, 91
Denville, Alfred, 134
Devant, David, 57
Diaghilev Ballet, 57
Dodd, Ken, 45, 137
Dolin, Anton, 101
Doonan, George, 98
Douglas of Kirtleside, Lord, 90
Douglass, R. H., 111
Dove, Alfred, 101
Dozin, Ivan, 128
Drake, Charlie, 141
Dryden, Leo, 110
Dublin, 38
Du Calion ("Duke"), 104-6
Duchess Theatre, Balham, 122
Dudley, Worcestershire, 15-16, 69
Dudley Empire, 25, 27, 28
Dudley Hippodrome, 28

Ealing Hippodrome, 122
Earle, Fred, 109
East Ham Palace, 126
Eastbourne Pier, 79, 133, 136
Edelsten, Ernest, 43
Edge, Jack, 130
Edinburgh, H.R.H. the Duke of, 90,
    91, 98-101
Edward VII, H.M. King, 72
Edwards, Jimmy, 124
Egbert, Albert, 93
Elen, Gus, 53, 110
Elliott, G. H., 54
Elmore, Belle, 29, 130
Elrick, George, 98
Elvin, Joe, 87, 88, 91, 109
Empire, Birmingham, 22
Empire, Croydon, 122, 126
Empire Theatre, Leicester Square, 107,
    108, 114, 117, 120
Era Annual Year Books, 27
Euston music-hall, 126
Evans, Dame Edith, 18
Evans, Norman, 45, 140

Fairburn, George, 87
Farren, Nellie, 21
Feldman, Bert, 48, 49
Fenston, Joseph, 89
Fields, Gracie, 44-5, 54, 80, 98, 101
Figaros, The, 110
Finck, Herman, 56
Finlay, Alec, 37
Finney, Albert, 18
Finney, James, 88
Finsbury Park Empire, 126, 139-40
Five Past Eight, 37
Flanagan, Bud, 86, 93, 98, 100, 103
Florence, Ada (Florence Venning),
    56-7
Forde, Florrie, 49, 80
Formby, George, Senior, 29, 34, 42
Formby, George, Junior, 42
Forrest, Arthur, 87
Forsyth, Bruce, 14, 22, 78, 137
Fournier, A. E. ("Bert"), 135
Fournier, Maurice, 135
Foux, William, 91
Fox, Olive, 38, 56, 57
Fox and Rose, 126, 128
Foy, Tom, 41
Fragson, Harry, 125
Frame, W. F., 37
Franks, Frank E., 40
Freeman, Harry, 23, 109
Friend, Violet, 28
Fyffe, Will, 36-7, 54, 78, 93

Gaiety Burlesques, 21
"Gaiety Girls, The" (Sisters Wynne), 110
Gaiety Theatre, Ayr, 38
Gaiety Whirl, 38
Gammon, Barclay, 124
Garner, Ernie, 33–5, 39
Gatti's restaurant, 112
Genée, Adele, 114
George V, H.M. King, 102, 103
Gibbons, Walter, 122
Gibbons' halls, 60
Gielgud, Sir John, 18
Gitana, Gertie, 80
Glasgow Empire, 75
Gordon, Harry, 37
Grace, W. G., 15
Grain, Corney, 125
Grand Theatre, Clapham, 122, 126
Granville, Walham Green, 126
Grenadier Guards bands, 16
Grey, Clifford, 50
Griffiths, Fred and Joe, 87
Grock, 57
Grossmith, George, Senior, 125
Guilbert, Yvette, 114
Guinness, Sir Alec, 18
Gulliver, Charles, 70

Hackney Empire, 63, 126
Half-Past-Eight, 38
Hallo Ragtime, 81
Hamilton, Russ, 141
Hammersmith Palace, 126
Hancock, Tony, 18
Hardwicke, Sir Cedric, *A Victorian in Orbit*, 17
Hargreaves, Bill, 51–2
Harmer, Dolly, 40
Harris, George, 87
Harris, Leslie, 125
Harrow Coliseum, 134
Hawthorn, Lil, 21
Hay, Will, 94, 101, 104
Hayman, John, 58
Haynes, Arthur, 14, 137
Henderson, Dick, 41
Henderson, Dickie, 38, 41, 86, 137
Henderson, Margot, 37, 137
Henlere, Herschel, 137
Herbert, Sir Alan P., 90
Hicks, Seymour, 57
Hockridge, Edmund, 137
Holborn Empire, 62, 126
Hollingshead, 21
Hopkins, Ted and May, 40
Horne, Brothers, 63
Houston, Renée, 37

Howerd, Frankie, 137, 141
Howes, Bobby, 99
Hunter, G. W., 110
Hunter, Jimmy, 79
Hurren, Dickie, 38
Hylton, Jack, 90, 93, 98, 101

Inge, Dean, 134
Irish Players (Abbey Theatre), 57
Irving, Henry, 73
Islington Empire, 126

Jackley, George, 93
Jackson, Nelson, 124–5
Jacobi, of the Alhambra, 56
Jaffa, Max, 86
James, Jimmy, 137, 142
Jay, Jack, 91
Jeans, Audrey, 86, 137
Jerome, Sidney, 86
Jewell, Jimmy, 99, 130–1
John Bull, 132
Jones, Hal, 66, 93
Jones, Tom, 40
Judge, Jack, 48

Karno, Fred, 94
Kaye, Danny, 103
Kemble, Larry, 101
Kenna, Con, 93
Kenyon, Neil, 34, 36
Keys, Nelson, 104, 105
Kilburn Empire, 62, 126
Kilby, Reginald, 86
King, Hetty, 128
King, Lester, 109
King's Theatre, Hammersmith, 133
Kingston Empire, 126
Kipling, Rudyard, 47, 111
Knowles, R. G., 79
Knox, Teddy, 99

Lacy, George, 38
Lafayette, The Great, 57
Lane, Jack, 41
Lashwood, George, 22
Lauder, Sir Harry, 33, 36, 49, 53, 59
Laye, Evelyn, 86
Learmouth, Jimmy, 39–40
LeBrunn, George, 52
Lee, Bert, 52–3
Leigh, Adele, 137
Leigh, Vivien, 18
Leighton, Queenie, 132
Lemprière, Lieutenant, 16
le Nève, Ethel, 29
Lenny the Lion, 142
Leno, Dan, 24, 27, 28, 73, 109, 110

Levy, Ethel, 81
Lewisham Hippodrome, 62, 126
Leybourne, George, 46
Little Tich, 13, 22, 33, 70, 101, 123
Liverpool, 77
Liverpool Hippodrome, 42
Lloyd, Hugh, 142
Lloyd, Marie, 21, 22, 54, 70-2, 80, 96, 110, 123
Lockwood, Johnny, 128
Loftus, Cissie, 22
Logan, Jimmy, 37
London Coliseum, 44, 57-61, 73, 101-3, 110, 126, 134
London Hippodrome, 70, 81, 96
London Palladium, 62, 110, 126, 127
London Pavilion, 21, 55
Long, Norman, 93
Loraine, Violet, 50
Lorimer, Jack, 36
Lorne, Tommy, 37
Lotto, Jack, 87, 88
L.T.V., 21, 60
Lucan, Arthur, 39
Luton Girls' Choir, 86
Lynn, Vera, 20, 50, 99

Macdermott, G. H., 46
Macdonnel, Leslie A., 91
McNab, Sandy, 30
MacNaghton Circuit, 21, 60-1, 127
McShane, Kitty, 39
Magonet, Dr. A. P., 90
Malcolm, Freddie, 93
Manchester: Opera House, 45, 70; Palace Theatre, 81
Marks, Alfred, 99, 136
Marlow, Harry, 129
Marlowe, Vic, 96
Martin, Millicent, 137
Mary, H.M. Queen, 44, 72, 102, 103
Massey, Anna, 18
Matthew, Billy, 128
Maxton, Jimmy, 134
May, Bobby, 96
Maynard, Bill, 142
Mayne, Clarice, 104
Melba, Dame Nellie, 17
Melville, Fred, 43
Melvin, G. S., 93
Metropolitan (the Met.), Edgware Road, 55, 126-8, 130
Miller, Eric, 91
Miller, Max, 135-6
Mills, Horace, 109, 110
Mills, Nat, 76, 100
Miners' Arms, The, Dudley, 31-3
Mitchell, Cooper, 124

Monks, Victoria ("John Bull's Girl"), 128
Moore, W. James, 91
Morecambe and Wise, 137
Morris, Harry, 14, 140
Morris and Cowley duo, 14, 140
Morton, Charles, 56, 57, 63
Moss Empires, 21, 34, 55, 127, 139
Murdoch, Richard "Stinker", 43
Murphy, C. W., 52

Nares, Owen, 57
National Association of Theatrical Employees, 122
Naughton and Gold, 99
Neatrour, Andrew, 91
Nerina, Nadia, 99
Nervo, Jimmy, 93
Nervo and Knox, 99
New Cross Empire, 126
Nicholls, Horatio (Lawrence Wright), 39
Nixon, David, 98, 99
Noni, 101
North, Rex, *The Butlin Story*, 139, 143
Novello, Ivor, 48

O'Connor, Des, 141
O'Dea, Jimmy, 38
O'Farrell, Talbot (Bill McIver), 39, 93
O'Gorman, Dave, 98, 124
O'Gorman, Joe, 124
Oliver, Vic, 99
Olivier, Sir Lawrence, 18
Olympia, Shoreditch, 126
On the Dole revue, 40
Osborne, Charles, 52
O'Toole, Dave, 93
O'Toole, Peter, 18
Oxford music-hall, 21, 55, 109-10

Palace Theatre, Shaftesbury Avenue, 56-7, 107, 111-12
Paragon, the, 21
Parnell, Val, 90
Peel, Mr., 116
Peers, Donald, 40-1
Penge Empire, 126
Persich, Jack, 60
Pertwee, Jon, 14, 99, 142
Pether, Henry, 52
Pickard, Helena, 17
Pickles, Wildred, 86, 99
Piemont Hotel, Soho Square, 113
Pinder, Powis, 42
Pink, Wal, 87, 88
Pinoli's restaurant, 107
Pleasants, Jack, 41-2

Pontin, F. W., 91
Poole, Brian, 142
Popplewell, Ben, 38
Popplewell, Eric and Leslie, 38
Potter, Gillie, 82-3
Powell, Sandy, 41, 99
Prince, Arthur, 57, 109
Pritchard, Tom, 28
Pub music-halls and concerts, 19, 20, 23
Putney Hippodrome, 111, 126

Queens, Poplar, 110

Radcliffe, Jack, 37
Rafferty, Pat, 38
Randall, Harry, 21
Ray, Ted, 14, 42, 86, 100, 128, 137
Redgrave, Sir Michael, 74
Redgrave, Vanessa, 18
Reece, Arthur, 46
Reeve, Ada, 22, 78
Regan, Joan, 20
Reid, Beryl, 34, 137
Reindeer, Eddie, 128
Rene, Ida, 57, 109
Rhodes, Dusty, 93
Richard, Cliff, 141
Rickaby, J. W., 52
Rigby, Arthur, 110
Riscoe, Johnnie, 77
Roberts, Arthur, 73, 79
Robey, George, 20, 33, 57, 69-70, 78, 96
Robinson, Cardew, 14, 95
Robson, Dame Flora, 18
Ross, Don, 80
Rotherhithe Hippodrome, 126
Roy, Derek, 14
Royal Automobile Club, 104-5
Royal Variety Performances, 71-2, 98-103
Russell, Fred, 87, 101, 111
Russell, Irene, 104
Ryland, Cliff, 29

Saintsbury, Kathleen, 74
Salberg, Derek, 38, 141
Sale, Jimmy, 56
Scatter, J. C., 39
Scofield, Paul, 18
Scott, Arthur and Betty, 129-30
Scott, Malcolm, 63-4
Scott, Sir Percy, 63
Scott, Terry, 142
Secombe, Harry, 18, 41, 99
Sellers, Peter, 18
Shand, Ernest, 35

Shanklin, 42, 82
Shapiro, Ted, 82
Shaw, Bernard, 133
Shaw, Lily, 109
Shelton, Anne, 20, 86, 99
Shepherds Bush Empire, 59, 126
Shields, Ella, 51, 104
Shufflewick, Mrs., 128
Sign of the Cross, The, 15
Smith, Clay, 132
South London Palace, 126
South Shields Empire, 88
Spicer, Dennis, 142
"Splinters", the, 66
Springfields, the, 142
Spurr, Mel B., 125
Squires, Rosemary, 142
Stage, The, 93, 123
Stanelli and Douglas, 101
Starr, Ringo, 142
Steele, Tommy, 137
Stennett, Stan, 142
Stewart, Andy, 37
Stirling, Sir Louis, 89
Stoll, Sir Oswald, 20, 46, 55, 57, 59-61, 63, 64, 106, 141, 143-4
Stoll Circuit, 127
Stoll Theatres, 139
Stone, Reg, 66
Stratford Empire, 126
Stratton, Eugene, 21, 22, 51, 54
Striptease shows, 66-7
Stuart, Leslie, 51
Sunday Night at the London Palladium, 22
Sunshine concert party, 42
Surrey Theatre, 122
Swaffer, Hannen, 90
Swinson, R. W., 124
Syndicate Halls, 21, 60, 139

Tate, Harry, 74-6, 92, 96, 104-5, 109, 130
Tate, Ronnie, 76, 92-3, 130
Taylor, Owen, 79
Tearle, Osmond, 16
Television Toppers, The, 99
Terriss, Ellaline, 57
Tetrazzini, 17
Theatre Royal, Birmingham, 44
Thorndike, Dame Sybil, 18, 19
Thorne, Ambrose, 64
Thorne, Dick, 88
Three Cheers revue, 49
Three Monarchs, The, 86
Tiller Girls, The, 99, 137
Tilley, Vesta, 53-4, 57, 72, 80
Tivoli, the, 21, 55
Tomlinson, Adam, 39

Tottenham Palace, 126
Train, Jack, 99
Tree, Mrs. H. Beerbohm, 111
Trinder, Tommy, 78, 79, 86, 99, 100,
   127, 130-1, 137
Tucker, Sophie, 81-2
Tutin, Dorothy, 18
Twinkle, 42, 64, 84, 129

Ustinov, Peter, 18

Valentine, Dickie, 99, 128, 137
Van Biene, 22
Vance, George, 46
Variety Artistes' Benevolent Fund,
   127, 129, 130
Variety Artistes' Federation, 111,
   122-4
Vaudeville Theatre, 132
Vaughan, Frankie, 14, 86, 99
Vaughan, Norman, 142
Vernon, Harriet, 21
Victoria, Queen, 15
Victoria Palace, 37, 58, 98, 126
Victoria Palace Girls, 101
Vinter, Harold, 144-5

Wakefield, Douglas, 93
Walham Green Empire, 126
Wall, Max, 36, 99
Wallace, Lionel, 116
Wallace, Nellie, 104
Wallis, Shani, 137

Walthamstow Palace, 126
Warriss, Ben, 86, 95, 98, 99, 130-1
Water Rats, The Grand Order of, 13,
   84-5, 87-91, 92-6, 98-101, 111, 143
Waters, Elsie and Doris, 79-80
Webber, E. Barry, 90
Webster, Sisters, 109
Wentworth, Bessie, 110
Weston, Bob, 52-3
Wheeler, Jimmy, 99, 130-1, 142
Whelan, Albert, 83-6, 98, 99, 104
Willesden Hippodrome, 126
Williams, Billy, 47
Williams, Bransby, 72-4
Willis, Dave, 37
Wilson, Victor, 127
Wilton, Robb, 44, 75-7
Windsor, Duke of, 104-5
Wisdom, Norman, 14, 78, 137
Wolfit, Sir Donald, 18
Wood, Wee Georgie, 40, 92, 96, 98,
   104
Woolwich Empire, 126
Wootwell, Tom, 22
Worsley, Arthur, 142
Worthing, 85, 129
Wright, Lawrence, 39
Wylie, Julian, 43
Wyndham, Fred, 37
Wynne, Sisters ("The Gaiety Girls"),
   110

Yana, 86, 99, 137